Pr

I have known Pastor Michael Bullock and his family for over thirty years and have seen the growth, faith, and love for his family increase through the years. As I read through the pages of this manuscript, I was moved by the honesty and openness of the pain and grief his family walked through with the death of his grandson, Miles. This is truly a prophetic book of encouragement and hope to all who have been in that place of despair and hopelessness. It will bring peace, comfort, and a promise of better things to come. Out of their darkness has come a light that will bring freedom to all who read it.

—Lois A. Hoshor
Author/Evangelist

Dr. Bullock . . . Michael . . . Mike . . . Beloved. The author, like the LORD, whittles down the woody contours of pastor hood, manhood, and fatherhood identity and, through the story of his daughter's great love loss, reveals the great faith-focusing force of Father love. No man's life, no matter how brief, is ever anonymous nor ever un-teaching. When we men are most vulnerable, like Mike and little Miles, we only then are able to experience trusting our perfect Father.

—Chip Weiant
Senior Fellow, Sagamore Institute
Project Director, Ohio GOOD Community and DADLAB
Board Member, Ohio Governor's Office of Faith-Based
& Community Initiatives

Everyone loses loved ones; few have invested their lives in preparing for it. Dr. Bullock imagined it and provided counseling for it, but when confronted with it, he, too, was challenged to identify why God mandates that we all experience it. Most of us (I did too) imagine life *without* loss; Pastor Bullock identifies the purpose for it. Thank you, friend.

—Mel Kurtz
President, Quasar Energy Group

After reading Pastor Bullock's book, *Even Now I Know,* and learning his thoughts, feelings, perceptions, and reflections, I feel that I have more awareness and appreciation for what women and their families go through when trying to understand and subsequently deal with the pain and loss of an unborn child.

—Donald Mason
Mayor, Zanesville, OH

Michael shares his family's emotional journey of love and loss in this poignant story. It is certain to resonate with those who have suffered similarly and found themselves questioning their faith and God's very existence. What unfolds is a triumph of hope, courage, and everlasting love revealed as healing begins and God's presence in our lives becomes evident once again.

—Congressman Troy Balderson
Representative from Ohio

Having preached in his church and been around Michael and his family, this is not an endorsement of a book; it is the endorsement of a life. My friend Michael is a pastor to pastors. This is not just a story; Michael invites us into raw moments of grief, reminding us God is far too wise to make a mistake and much too kind to be cruel. *Even Now I Know* will bring healing to a hardened heart and restore courage to persevere through our own dark seasons of pain. Michael reminds us time is not the healer of all wounds. Instead, it is Jesus and being in the Word of God every day that truly brings restoration to our innermost hurt and insight into our most perplexing questions in life.

—Dr. Samuel M. Huddleston
Assistant District Superintendent, Assemblies of God,
Northern California & Nevada
Executive Presbyter, Assemblies of God, USA

A must-read as Pastor Michael takes us through his family's heartbreaking journey of grief. His message that 'You may not understand today or tomorrow, but eventually God will reveal why you went through everything you did' resonates and imparts comfort that we do not have to understand to trust God. He gives insight into how everyone has pain and something to deal with and equips us to deal with it when it comes our way. His transparency in dealing with his personal struggles and family's heartache may be his best ministry yet!

—Rye D'Orazio
Executive Director, Central Ohio FCA
(Fellowship of Christian Athletes)

EVEN NOW I KNOW

EVEN NOW I KNOW

Michael Bullock, D.Min.

ethos
collective

Published by Ethos Collective™
PO Box 43, Powell, OH 43065
EthosCollective.vip

LCCN: 2023907593
Paperback ISBN: 978-1-63680-166-7
Hardback ISBN: 978-1-63680-167-4
e-book ISBN: 978-1-63680-168-1

Available in paperback, hardback, and e-book

Through pain and loss, this book is dedicated to our beloved Miles. He inspired the words on these pages and will forever be loved. And though his life on this earth was for but a moment, his impact will be eternal.

Table of Contents

Introduction

Even Now I Know is a book about our family's journey in recovering from the loss of our beloved Miles Owen Moore. Miles was stillborn, or as his mother called it, he was born sleeping. While this is an unfortunate experience for our family, we know many other families who, for decades, have had to battle back from the pain and loss of a child in the same manner. This book is about grief and healing. It is about faith, frustration, and God's ability to help his children in times of need. Also, it addresses the question of where God is in our time of intense pain. The book delves into the details of the dark days as our daughter, Jennifer, found her way back into the light of God's grace. It tackles questions of faith and fairness in life. But it also addresses ways in which hope can be found again. *Even Now I Know* shares how you can live again and find purpose from your loss. And unapologetically, this book shares our faith in Christ as the one who pulled us up into life again.

This is also a book sharing a parallel story of Martha's experience with Jesus as she engages in a conversation with him after the death of her brother Lazarus. It was in her words that I found comfort, even if I didn't find answers. In sharing Martha's words and experience, and in sharing our family's words and experience, I hope others will be able to find comfort in the unanswerable questions of grief, sorrow, pain, and uncertainty. The words on the following pages are not designed to be clinical, nor are they designed to provide some theologically deep insight. The words are only my attempt to share God's heart with those who have hurt as we have hurt and to help those who are still searching for answers.

My prayer for you, as it has been for our family, is for all of us to be able to know these three simple truths:

1. Life has situations we may never be able to explain.
2. Tragedy and pain affect us all.
3. God's love is not based on our circumstances and chaos but is available through them.

Thank you for taking the time to read through our journey as we together find peace and resolution in the grace of Christ through the presence of the Spirit, as given by the love of our heavenly Father.

ONE

Unintended Situations

Grief never ends . . . but it changes. It's a passage, not a place to stay. Grief is not a sign of weakness, nor a lack of faith . . . it is the price of love.

—Unknown

October 10, 2021, started out as a normal Sunday morning. I was sitting in my church office, listening to the conversations happening as people were arriving for our morning church service. Kids were giggling, adults greeted one another, and I scanned my sermon notes half-heartedly, which is all part of the Sunday morning routine. But on this morning, I would soon find out it wasn't going to be a normal Sunday morning.

Every Sunday, congregants enter by one of two entrances. They arrive either by our two front doors or through our side door, which is protected from the weather by a carport.

Those who enter from the carport may stop in our café for a morning beverage or pastry before our worship service. I have an open door, and often people will stop and say hello or want to share in conversation because we have not seen each other throughout the week. This is why reviewing my sermon notes half-heartedly is part of the Sunday morning process. That way, unannounced interruptions are allowable because I am not deeply entrenched in my thoughts.

This practice has only been for the past several years after we moved from one building location to another due to our church's growth. However, as we began to grow, it became apparent that I was having to stretch spiritually. More importantly, I had to grow in my leadership role as we took on more staff and more responsibilities. Increasing personal development and improving one's skills is never an easy thing. It doesn't matter what area you must develop because all growth requires stretching. Stretching and improving may produce an element of pain, which, in turn, leads to some kind of change.

There are times when growing can be calculated and intentional. You go to leadership classes or read books on how to become a better leader or a better person. Or you can sit and learn from others who are able to help you in your own setting by giving you tools and wisdom to aid you along the way. But then there are the unintentional situations catching you off guard—those moments in life and ministry that weren't planned. They cause you to respond in a manner that exposes your level of leadership and the areas in which you need improvement. It is the latter part of this, the unintended situation, which hit me and our family on this day. A situation was happening to stretch me, grow me as a leader, and force me to recognize my weakness as a man. An unannounced and unrehearsed day forever etched in my memory. It changed the complexion of our family as we were confronted with the ensuing news.

Feelings change . . . memories don't.
—Joel Alexander

It was getting close to ten o'clock, the time our church service began. Our youngest daughter, Jennifer, came into my office with a different look on her face. At first, I didn't think anything of it. She was thirty-three weeks pregnant. Her hormones were fluctuating. Her body was changing. But then, with tears in her eyes, she uttered the words that changed her life, her family's life, our family's lives, and our future in a way we never anticipated. She tearfully said, "Daddy, he's gone!" My first thought was, *who's gone? And where did he go?* This was the first thing occupying my mind. Then I asked her what she meant. It was at that moment my heart sank to a depth I had never felt nor known existed. "My baby boy, he's dead; I just know it. He hasn't moved since 1:00 a.m. this morning, and I know he is dead."

Mind you, the noise and chatter continued to escalate from outside my office. It didn't drown out or cover up the deep-seated sinking in the pit of my stomach I felt at that moment. Of course, as her father, I tried to comfort and reassure her in a lame attempt, stating she didn't know for sure and that it could be something else at this point. As her pastor, I tried to remain stoic and reassure her God always knows things we don't, and everything would be fine. As a man, I couldn't understand what all women know, what all women feel in carrying a life—the innate sense of what their child is doing and how the child is lying in their womb. I can't begin to have any insight as to the connection felt as a mother and child connect even beyond the umbilical cord.

There is an emotional, spiritual, physical, and psychological connection that moms and babies have, and men cannot comprehend. As a man, I could only empathize with the situation and compartmentalize it because I still had a job to do.

Men don't always connect in challenging situations with an emotional appeal. We segment and put our thoughts and emotions into boxes. We start to think of ways to fix what is broken without attaching ourselves emotionally or physically. We operate differently, which is how God created us. We sometimes function more out of duty than out of discretion. For me, I had to get to the sanctuary. We had people coming to church to worship. They were now coming in as waves with their own problems and needs. We had a service to attend to with singing, offering, announcements, and youth church. And, of course, I had to preach. I had to put on my pastor's hat. I had to close my daddy's box and open the lid to my preacher's box. I couldn't stand in front of our congregation and preach the sermon I had prepared with thoughts of my daughter on my mind, or so I thought.

As I headed to the sanctuary, Jennifer (Jenn, as we call her) continued sitting in my office, as per my instruction. She eventually made her way into the sanctuary as the worship music started. I don't know if you have ever experienced an internal silence amid the external noise, but in that span of our worship, I heard the songs and sang them with my lips, but my mind asked questions that challenged the speed of sound. I asked, *Lord, what is happening? What's going on? Make this a bad mistake; don't let this happen. We can't go through this. How can I preach?* Like the Energizer Bunny™, these thoughts continued pounding the drum in my mind as the conversation kept scrolling forward in my head. My wife, Kathy, was standing behind me with tears streaming down her face, praising Jesus in song at the top of her lungs. Our other daughter, Pamela, Jenn's older sister, was being her efficient and supportive self by trying to corral the other children, our grandchildren, Michael, Noah, and Harper. The music continued as all of this played out, both in slow motion and in real time. I felt uneasy, yet surreal. I don't ever want to relive that experience. I asked the Lord never to put us in this situation again.

The music stopped. It was my time to proceed to the platform. It seemed as if the stage were further away this morning. There were hundreds of times I had made my way to the platform, but on this day, it was different—it was more difficult. Yet, gathering myself, I turned and faced our congregation of worshippers. Smiling, projecting a joy I knew they needed to see. I tried to maintain a sense of being spiritual at that moment. I hoped the congregation was unable to sense my being engaged deeply within my own thoughts and almost completely disengaged from them.

When Duty Calls

The first order of business when I enter the pulpit is to dismiss the children to junior church. I looked over in the front row to see Jenn still sitting there. Normally, she goes down to help with our youth ministry, but not this morning, not this day, and not this time.

The sermon went forward, with my mouth moving and my mind trying to stay focused on the message at hand. I think I heard a few amens and agreements of approval. But on this day, none of it mattered. Everything happened as if I were in some tunnel. My voice reverberated in my head. I heard my voice, but I wasn't listening to myself. I could see the people, but their faces weren't there; they were images and figures. I couldn't make eye contact with anyone, yet I saw them all. And still, the entire time, I was trying not to look over at Jenn, though I was compelled as her father, to look anyway.

If you have ever had an unexpected situation in your life, then you may understand how, at times, duty calls. You may not be able to stop life, even if an unexpected situation stops you in your tracks. September 11, 2001, for many Americans, was one of those times. We stopped for a moment but had to continue living with one eye on our duty and one eye on the television screen. We were trying to make sense of a senseless act and numbly trying to figure out what was going on in this unexpected period in history. This Sunday morning was my 9/11, if you will, my unexpected moment of having to preach and trying to be a father.

Then, somewhere along the way, the message stopped. Jenn had left during the closing prayer to avoid being confronted by anyone or having to talk to anyone. I wish people knew the pressures of having eyes on you all the time. Being watched, looked at, pulled on, and constantly having to be on top of your game. It's the nature of being in ministry as a pastor and family. It is also part of the life Jenn has made for herself, based on her work and the environment she lives in.

No matter how bad your heart is broken,
the world doesn't stop for your grief.
—Faraaz Kazi

Jenn is a news anchor at a major television station in Columbus, Ohio. Her pregnancy included a public announcement on air that was met with cheers and congratulations. Over the succeeding months, she would intermittently give updates. Eventually, she couldn't hide her baby bump or the glow from carrying a child. It was all being played out on Facebook, her news shows, in her city, and her hometown of Zanesville every weekend when she and her sister would come home for church. Because of Jenn's notoriety, Kathy and I were also congratulated. People in our church and community were watching her on the news or following her on social media. We felt the eyes and smiles and enjoyed thinking of how our family continued to grow.

Within six years, we gained two sons-in-law and three grandchildren and moved into a new church building. Like the rest of the world, we had navigated through the COVID pandemic. Kathy had gone through an unexpected heart attack, and I had nineteen inches of my intestine removed during bowel-resection surgery. We celebrated thirty years of being in ministry, and now we were preparing for a new grandchild. Life was good, challenging, and moving at the speed of God. Our church was growing, and my duties both to the church and our community grew as well.

Because of the pandemic, to stay in touch with our church folks, my brother-in-law suggested I do a two-to-three-minute hello to the people via Facebook (something I have finally forgiven him for). At my age, making videos on Facebook was not my cup of tea, nor was I adept at using Facebook. But I began what is known as Wednesday Word. It was just a weekly pick-me-up, which began to spread rapidly throughout our people who shared it with their family and friends. On Wednesday Word, I shared the good news of Jenn's pregnancy and the journey of our ministry. It was a time of blessing and joy. Whenever the girls came to the house, chaos ensued. Michael, Noah, and Harper somehow dismantled our entire home within a matter of hours. But it was all fun and happiness for thirty-two weeks. But then, on Sunday, October 10, life hit us hard.

As Jenn left the sanctuary, she abruptly ducked into my office and closed the door. I continued to greet the people, then said my goodbyes, making sure everyone was gone and out of the church before opening my office door. By that time, Kathy was already in my office, along with Pamela and all the kids. The discussion was whether to do our usual dinner at Grandma's house (Kathy's mom) or if Jenn, Pamela, and the kids should go straight back to Columbus. To her credit, Jenn went to Grandma's house to eat, visit, and sit in quiet contemplation, unsure of what was happening. But at the same time, she had a sense of what was happening with her baby.

An hour had passed while at Grandma's. Finally, Jenn couldn't take it any longer. She and Pamela loaded the kids in the van and headed to Columbus. She had called ahead to her husband, Gerald, and her OB-GYN to get some sense of what to do next. Kathy and I went home. This was one of the quietest Sunday evenings we had ever spent together. Every time I looked over at Kathy, I could see her lips moving. She was praying. What else does a mother do in a situation like this? What does anyone do in circumstances like these? I cannot tell you at this point what we had for dinner or what we watched on television. We both sat with phones nearby, waiting for news and some information. In suspenseful situations, time seems to drag on forever. When you are having fun, laughing, and feeling full of life, time speeds up, and those moments quickly fly by. But when you are agonizing in anticipation of news, you can feel the slow progression of time. You look at your watch or your phone repeatedly. You try to busy yourself, but time still creeps along at a snail's pace. You then have no other choice but to keep waiting. We knew Jenn and Gerald were at the hospital. Pamela had Noah and Harper (Jenn's other two children) along with her husband, Kendall, and her son, Michael. We were all waiting, hoping, praying, and, yes, begging God for good news or at least some news giving us cause to breathe again.

Not All News Is Good News

At some point, we went to bed and woke up on Monday morning, October 11, 2021. I typically don't go into the office on Monday mornings; I wait until the afternoon to take a mental break from Sunday's service. On this Monday, Kathy was home. She wasn't traveling, and because of the pandemic, she and many of her co-workers had been working from home. Pretty much like the rest of America and its workforce, she was learning how to do Zoom meetings. Around 9:00 a.m., Kathy's phone rang. I don't remember all the conversation, but I do recall Kathy saying, "Hey, Jenn." From there, the only other words I remember were, "Oh, Jenn, I am so sorry." I know she shared more in the conversation, but in those few minutes, my senses grew numb. I heard Kathy talking, but it was muffled. There are times (some call them unspoken moments) when you know something, even if you don't know the specifics of it. You can tell when something is wrong by the tone of voice, facial expression, or in this instance, both. Plus, tears began to flow down Kathy's cheeks. She put the phone down, turned to me, and said, "He's gone. He didn't live." Jenn had lost the baby. He was stillborn.

As the words came off Kathy's lips, my mind went blank. Have you ever been punched in the gut by such traumatic news that you go blank? Have you ever been told something that created an emptiness in your belly? There I was, standing in nowhere land, feeling nauseated and unnerved. *How do I process this? How do any of us process such news? This wasn't supposed to happen. How did this happen? Were there warning signs? Did the doctors miss something?* My mind flooded with questions and concerns. I couldn't think straight, nor could I think clearly. We had just been given the news of why Jenn went back to Columbus. And it was not good news.

TWO

The Price We Pay

From the end of the earth, I will cry to You, when my heart is overwhelmed; lead me to the Rock that is higher than I.

—Psalm 61:2 (NKJV)

eing a pastor has been both the most amazing thing in my life and, at the same time, the most painful. Unless you have truly been called by God, it is hard to know the highs and lows of pastoring. You won't fully understand the dynamics of being the voice of the Lord and a leader of his people. Like a man who cannot understand pregnancy, most people don't understand what pastors go through and endure every day. Most of what we deal with are other people's problems. We conduct weddings and funerals and see grief and sorrow regularly. We counsel and advise on subjects that we may not be experts in but do so because we love our people, God's people. When tragedy hits us, we don't have anyone else to turn to. We, in most cases, stand alone and lean on our spouses.

As Kathy turned to me and said those painful words about Jenn losing Miles, all I could do was hold her and let her cry on my shoulder. At the time, we had been married for thirty-eight years. I have seen my wife cry many times. She cried as she lost family members: her grandparents, her dad, and her younger brother Gregg. She cried over members of our church whom she loved. Kathy has cried many times but never like this. Now she cried for her baby girl and her grandson. This was a shock to the entire system of the body. Your mind is frozen in time, and your heart has not only been broken but shattered. Your emotional tank starts running, and eventually, it hits empty. And your spirit, the most important part of your being, has just been hit with a jolt that would bring even the most diehard, faith-filled saint to the place of utter despair. In our kitchen, I held my wife, my best friend, and my partner in life. She cried and cried until, finally, her tear ducts needed a break.

The whole time she cried, I simply stood there, holding her, unable to think or process what was happening. It seemed more like I was pondering and searching for answers than anything. Eventually, Kathy was able to gather herself. She paused in the depth of her tears long enough to ask me how I was doing. I hadn't cried or even made a sound. I remember saying something like, "I don't know." I was still dazed and lost in my questions. Then I did what most men do. I walked out of the house, went to our garage, got my lawn mower, and proceeded to cut the grass.

Most men will not tell you, even if they have not realized, that they have a common fear. They have a fear of failure. It is part of a man's DNA. We fear failing our families. We fear losing our jobs because we are valued for what we do.

We fear not measuring up to society's requirements and standards. What we do then is try to fix things. Men have an innate desire to try to fix things. Anything and everything, it doesn't matter. And if we can't fix it, then we find someone else who can. Because it must be fixed, or else we fail. Cutting grass, in that instant, seemed the most logical thing to do because I could fix my yard—I could make it look better. Cutting the grass would make me feel as if I had accomplished something.

As I pushed my mower across the grass, I made sure my lines were straight. I paid attention to my rows while my brain was in overdrive, spinning feverishly. I was trying to process the best way I knew how, which was to put on my pastor's hat and go into my pastor's box even though it was a Monday. The pastor part of me leads me into spiritual matters. It allows me to deal with God stuff. Stuff that is faith-believing, miracle-working, raising-people-from-the-dead kind of stuff. From Elijah and Elisha to Jesus, I tried to recall all the resurrections of the Bible. Could God be getting ready to do a miracle in our family, for our church, and for the world to see? Maybe this was something of biblical proportions. Was this a test of my faith, our faith, for me to breathe on my grandson and see him come to life? Perhaps I was to speak to the proverbial mountain and see the miracle of all miracles, a life resurrected. With Bible verse after verse and story after story, my pastoral mind was racing.

I've dealt with death many times, have done my fair share of funerals, and sat with grieving families who had lost loved ones. But none of those events were like this. Only a few years prior, I had lost my youngest brother, Chuckie, and met the challenge of having to do his funeral with a spiritual fervor and faith that only those in the pastoral profession can truly understand and appreciate. I loved my brother. Doing his funeral was extremely difficult. But this was different. This was my grandson, my daughter, and a pain our family had never experienced before.

Sister Act

Talking to your sister is sometimes all the therapy you need.
—Unknown Author

At this point, I must interject that our daughter Pamela, Jenn's big sister, had experienced a miscarriage just the year before. In October 2020, she lost her baby after eight weeks. It was a traumatic experience for her. At the time, her mother and I didn't fully understand the situation. What we eventually learned, from Pamela's vantage point, was the loss of Miles carried more guilt for her. She, as the protective sister, became angrier at her baby sister's heartache than her very own.

For some unknown reason, we don't treat miscarriages in the same manner as a stillbirth. A stillborn child is real. A stillborn child has been born from its mother's womb. These children are born sleeping, looked upon, held, kissed, felt, and cuddled. There is a realness to seeing and experiencing a child born sleeping that produces a different grief. Maybe this is because, as a society, we've allowed the abortion issue to numb us from the truth: a life inside a belly is as much of a life as one outside the belly. For a woman, the trauma of losing a child, whether by birth or during her pregnancy, is still traumatic and heart-wrenching. And now Pamela had to go through this with her baby sister, stepping up and supporting her, all the while having gone through her own trauma with little acknowledgment and support.

If there is anything I have learned through this experience, it is that loss is loss, no matter the stage. A miscarriage has as much sting and hurts as much as any other loss. The mental anguish and emotional toll the loss takes on a mother is not to be dismissed. For a father, the mental loss and emptiness of being unable to fix the pain cuts deep. His grief over a miscarriage is real as well. Neither should be overlooked. Whether you have suffered a loss or not, simply saying that you don't understand what it feels like is not acceptable.

What a champion of an older sister Pamela is. She set her own hurt aside, her own memories and pain, to tend to the needs of her little sister.

Still No Answers

I can't promise to fix all your problems, but I can promise you won't have to face them alone.
— Unknown Author

Our yard has two sides to it. There is the side our house sits on and the other side, next to our neighbors. Between the two yards is an asphalt driveway dissecting our property. I finished cutting the grass on the side our house sits on. Taking a break, as I always do even when things are normal, I sat down on the porch. Kathy came out, no longer crying but showing tear tracks on her face. Her eyes were puffy and carried a sadness I had never seen before. She placed her hand on my back and asked me again, "How are you doing?" I still didn't know. I was still in pastor mode, feeling the pain of our loss and the sting of the situation but having to steady myself. At some point, I would need to find the right words to say. And as a preacher of the gospel, I would need to find the right Bible verse to recite. I would have to draw upon my years of education and experience in pastoring, remember all the lessons on how to handle the onslaught of questions people would ask, and do it with a smile on my face, fighting hard not to show personal pain and hurt. I said again to Kath (my pet name for her), "I don't know."

She, however, knew it wasn't true. She knew me better than anyone. She knows when I am hiding my feelings when I am in retreat mode. I am the answer man—the guy most people came to for answers dealing with the deep questions of faith and life as well as trivial questions like where a bible verse was located. At that moment, I was being a pastor, hiding my true feelings because we are to be strong, stoic, and steady examples of godly men. Pastors don't talk about our feelings or share our emotions, especially in front of our congregations or in public. We represent God in all we do, as well as our family, our congregation, and our community. We live, or at least we are supposed to live, at a higher standard. We feel obligated to remain emotionless for as long as possible. Even when we get bad family news, we don't know how to react. As a man from my generation as a boomer, you just didn't talk about these things. Real men don't cry, as the saying goes. You worked with your hands, steeled your mind, cut grass, and didn't share how you truly felt. You just don't do those things as men.

After a few minutes of sitting in silence, I went back to my mower and my yard. The other side of my yard is oblong. It's about twenty-five yards wide and forty yards long (I've measured). It was at the fifteen-yard mark of length, and I was still checking my lines and the stripes as I made sure they were straight. This was when the transition from pastor to father started to kick in. I'm not sure how, but my pastor's hat was falling off, and my daddy's hat was taking its place. I was closing one box and opening another, and I could sense something stirring deep inside me. A deep-down guttural cry rose from my stomach. Tension gripped me. My mind was no longer on my call as a pastor. All I could do was think about both my baby girl and my born-sleeping grandson.

THREE

God Didn't Give Me Boys

Little by little, we let go of loss . . . but never of love.

—Unknown

For those who don't know me, my girls were both daddy's girls. I told them from the moment I knew Kathy was pregnant that I loved them. This was important because of my upbringing. The words "I love you" were hardly spoken, if at all, while I grew up. Love was not commonplace, nor was it within my understanding. Not just a godly kind of love but love in general. Not even the romantic-movie kind of love, the boy-meets-girl kind, with the music playing in the background and the fields of flowers glistening below a sunlit sky.

Kathy and her family taught me about affectionate love—the kind of love where you have feelings towards another in a non-sexual and unconditional way. God, knowing my personality, blessed me with two girls who taught me the deeper meaning of the word. The Bible calls it agape. It is a deep, unconditional, selfless expression from one person to another. Boys would not have taught me that lesson. I think maybe boys would have brought out the wrong side of my personality as well as the ugly parts of my temper. My girls helped me to become a better man by teaching me restraint, patience, and calmness. Especially when they began to date, the word restraint took on a whole new meaning. As a girl dad, I learned how to braid hair, strap on patent leather shoes, tie perfect bows on frilly dresses, sit through dance recitals, go on school field trips, and cook beanie weenies (still their favorite after-school meal to this day).

My girls, however, were able to throw me a bone. They were both tremendous athletes in their respective sports. It allowed me to have a sense of what being a father of boys would feel like without all the extra yelling and screaming (I only did a little with them). I love my girls. They are the crown of all my life has been. Don't get me wrong; the grandchildren are the jewels in the crown. But without my girls, there would be no grandchildren. They are still Daddy's girls. I still do anything for them, and for as long as I am able and capable, I will.

And suddenly, while cutting that small section of grass, I began to think of my girls and their pain. And more intimately, of Jenn and her loss. I couldn't fathom what she was going through, and worse, I couldn't fix it. The straight lines of my lawn suddenly meant nothing. Trying to mow perfect rows became futile. I was spending my energy on holding in my emotions and feelings, or so I thought I was.

More in the Kitchen than Appliances

I couldn't stop my thought process. Everything in my mind was about my girls and, more specifically, about Jenn. Transitioning from pastor to father, from required duties to relational daddy, the emotions began to take effect. There was a compulsion for me to let go of my emotions. Instead, the compulsion resulted in my letting go of my mower. Fortunately, my mower has one of those second bars, so when you release the handle, the mower automatically shuts off. The mower did as it was supposed to; it shut off. But that's when I began to feel my heart, and the tears turned on. A deep, guttural cry rose in my belly. If you have ever cried hard, real hard, you know what I mean. You feel it, and you know you can't stop it. No matter how hard you try, you can't keep it down. It rises and overtakes you.

I started walking briskly towards the house. Kathy had gone back inside by now. I reached our side door, the kitchen door, opened it as quickly as possible, and without any steps, lunged forward and fell face-first on the kitchen floor. I did not trip, nor did I try to fling myself—I collapsed. I couldn't fix this. I couldn't be there for Jenn. I had failed Pamela by not realizing her pain, and now I was failing Jenn. Deeply entrenched in the pain of the moment, I sobbed. My mouth cried out, "My baby girl, my baby boy!" I asked God—rather, I demanded God—to tell me why. No longer was I wearing my pastoral cap. This was a father, a daddy, asking and begging for an answer as to why this was happening to his baby girl. I lay there on the kitchen floor, pouring out real tears, crying so hard and deeply that my stomach rose and fell with every heave. The intensity of it was nothing like I had ever felt before.

To Everything, There Is a Season, Including Crying

Those we love don't go away; they walk beside us every day.
—Alex MacLean

After my brother Chuckie died, I was honored to officiate his funeral. For the entire time, from his death until the closing prayer of his funeral, I held it together. I didn't cry or even shed a single tear. But as we were finishing up the end of his funeral service, I took Kathy's hand and went into the office of the funeral director and cried. I was ingrained in the emotional loss of my baby brother. But even then, it was only for a few minutes, and I was done.

Crying for Jenn and Miles was different. It was sustained, enduring, and deeper. With Chuckie, I had some ideas as to why I cried. I also had forty-seven years of being his brother, him being alive and being a part of my life. This was different. Miles was unexpected and unrehearsed. The pastor in me was now sitting somewhere in another room. It wasn't until later that the possibility of my taking off my pastoral robe occurred to me. Never had I separated my role as pastor from my blessing as a father. I am not sure if others have ever struggled in this way. But at that moment, I was completely empty and void of anything resembling being a pastor. The father in me had taken over fully, and he had many questions for God.

Why God? Why did this happen? What are you doing to our family? We have given you our full attention, our lives. I gave up being in the corporate world to be a lowly preacher, the guy that everyone jokes about only working one day a week. People invade his privacy, but when he needs someone else, they are nowhere to be found. I've been the guy who, by nature of people's assumption, must be in church every Sunday, or he's regarded as not doing his job and not earning his paycheck. God, we have served you, served the church you planted, served the people you gave us, and served the community You put us in. We have set aside our lives to serve you, and now you do this to us. I am angry, I am bitter, and I am deeply frustrated with you. If I had known this would happen in our future, I never would have said yes to the call. I never would have said yes to starting a church. I never would have put my wife and children through all the hurt and ridicule of things we've had to endure being in ministry. I would not have done any of it, and even now, I am ready to quit because you allowed this to happen.

As I continued to lie there in pain and anguish, tears pooled on the floor in front of me. My stomach heaved. By now, Kathy had come into the kitchen. I don't know what was on her mind. I don't know what she was thinking, seeing her husband lying there. The man she knew as her strength collapsed on the kitchen floor, her solid foundation now resolute and empty of his manhood. But then I felt her touch. She put her hand on my back. I know she wanted me to know she was there. But she couldn't console me or answer my questions. She could only sit there next to me. Like a pastor at the side of a grieving family, she sat there. Then, somewhere within that moment, she found more tears. Kathy joined in my pain. She lay next to the father of her children on the same kitchen floor. Both of us were weakened by the moment, overcome by our helplessness. But she couldn't experience my sense of failure. Like a man cannot comprehend pregnancy, a woman cannot comprehend a man's depletion of success. Yet she sat with me, not over me, not just beside me, but with me. Not just in her pain but in my pain as well. She has journeyed through this adult life with me. She was there when I confronted my parents about my adoption. Kathy was there when I lost my brother, when I had all my surgeries, and when I spent countless hours away from home earning my degrees. She has always been there, not just beside me, but with me, feeling as deeply as I felt. But at this moment, she was a woman who could not understand the failure of her man, who was lying there, weeping profusely, failing miserably, and now questioning a God who has always been there for him.

As quickly as I fell to the ground, I stood. I grabbed the hand towel that I used to wipe away the sweat from my face when cutting the grass. Now, I used it to wipe away my tears. Without fanfare or words, I hugged Kath, walked out of the house, and finished cutting the grass. I could still fix my yard. I could still accomplish something. I could still avoid being a complete and total failure.

I don't remember much about the rest of the day. At one point, Kathy told me the reason we hadn't heard from Jenn earlier was that they had to do a total hysterectomy. She was in recovery from the procedure and unable to call. Apparently, Miles' placenta was entrenched in her uterus. To save her life, Miles had to give up his. This made no sense. With all the medical advancements we have, all the technology, and all the equipment available, wasn't there something within those ultrasounds that would have shown what was happening? And why at thirty-three weeks? Why did this have to happen at all, and what stupid lesson was God trying to teach us? Yes, I know; everyone in life goes through things. Everyone has something they deal with. Yes, I know women have been losing children since time began, and it is a difficult part of life.

But this was our family, the people who served the Lord. The people who gave up so much to do his will. Jenn had been through two ablation procedures to cauterize a portion of her heart caused by supraventricular tachycardia, or SVT. (When SVT kicks in, it causes the electrical pathway to go in a different direction, and then the electrical current sends a signal, causing your heart rate to speed up, causing atrial fibrillation or A-fib.) Her first ablation procedure was at age twelve, and her second was at age twenty-two. From age six to now, she has been on medication. *Again, God, why her? Why did she have to give up her son at thirty-three weeks? Why were you putting on her one more thing, one more trauma, one more bad situation? Why did she have to give up her baby boy? Did he have to die?* In the conversation I was having in my head, something hit me with suddenness and a bang: thirty-three weeks. Why does that number stand out to me? And there it was. A mini revelation to the myriad of questions I had been asking God. It didn't change the situation, nor did it ease the pain, but it was something he knew I needed at that instant. A mini revelation of heavenly proportions.

FOUR

Weeks Are More than Seven Days

*You may not understand today or tomorrow, but eventually
God will reveal why you went through everything you did.*

—Unknown

The pastoral part of me had a revelation, even if the
father part of me was still numb and in denial. My mini
revelation was how our heavenly Father gave up his Son
for the entire world at age thirty-three. The apostle John
tells us that "God so loved the world that he gave his one
and only Son, that whoever believes in him shall not perish
but have eternal life" (John 3:16, NIV). Somewhere within
the spiritual realm of this verse, my pastoral side was trying
to make sense of it all. Thirty-three weeks is not the same

as thirty-three years, but Miles was not the Son of God. He was Jenn and Gerald's son. For some unknown reason, he gave up his life for his mom, his dad, his siblings, his cousins, his aunt and uncle, and his grandparents. For some reason, he had to go straight to Heaven while we lived in pain here on Earth.

Thirty-three weeks doesn't seem like a long time compared to thirty-three years. But when you are tracking the growth of a child during pregnancy, every conversation is precious. Seeing the ultrasound images of the unborn baby creates excitement, enthusiasm, and anticipation. Discovering the baby's gender and the progression of seeing a life being formed are indescribable joys. All who have experienced these activities know exactly what I am talking about. But not all have to experience the unexpected pain of having a stillbirth. Only a select few can comprehend how long thirty-three weeks last. Only a select few can say they gave birth to a child born sleeping.   Miles must have truly loved Jenn. With his placenta attached to her uterus, the doctors had to make a choice: the baby or the mommy. What a horrible position for them. God had to make a choice: his people or his Son. He chose his Son to be the sacrifice for people. Miles was chosen to be the sacrifice so his mommy could go on living. Miles chose to keep me from losing him *and* my little girl.

I tried to make sense of this horrendous part of our family's life. I tried to busy my mind with why it happened. But it didn't change the fact that it happened. For the rest of the day, Kathy and I didn't speak much. Words wouldn't bring comfort, nor would they produce answers. I'm sure there was a Monday Night Football game on television, but I couldn't tell you who played, and quite frankly, I didn't care.

Silence Isn't Golden

All men by nature desire knowledge.
—Aristotle

It's amazing how the mind works in tragic situations. We, as humans, need answers. We need to figure things out. And as a man, I needed to figure it out so I could fix what I could fix. We need to have information and knowledge to solve problems, deal with situations, or make sense of the senseless. That's life as a human being. We deal in the physical realm, the things we can touch, taste, smell, hear, or see. We don't dwell much in the spiritual realm. It requires us to tap into an area that isn't always tangible.

I don't know how others deal with bad situations, but I shut down. When I don't understand something or don't like what's happening, I get quiet, reserved, and withdrawn. In those moments, I am processing, trying to problem-solve, but mostly reflecting. To some, it looks as if I am disinterested or disengaged, but truthfully, I am deep in thought and my emotions and trying to keep them in check. Others may be more expressive and show outward signs of their turmoil. Kathy gets busy doing things. Not so much cleaning the house, just doing things: looking at our bills, doing all the laundry, picking up toys from the grandkids, or straightening up around the house. That Monday, she was staying active, staying busy, and trying not to cry. Kathy was fighting to keep her mind from wandering in torment and struggling because she couldn't get to know her little girl, her baby, to hold her and tell her everything would be okay.

God has a reason for everything, even if we don't know what it is or doesn't make any sense to us. We couldn't put our finger on it or describe it in detail, but we knew there was a reason. We didn't have to like it. But we had to accept it. Through our many years of walking with the Lord, we knew. And we knew God knew. We don't like it now, and we didn't like it then, but we knew in some grander scheme of things, God had a plan, and he would provide the answers when the time was warranted and when we were ready. This knowledge brought enough peace to make it through the night.

Sleep that night didn't come and stay for very long. The next day, we called the hospital, talked to Gerald, and then sat at home. I don't remember much about that day either, other than it was a Tuesday. Word hadn't gotten out yet, so we were still, as a family, caught up in our own sorrow and pain. Kathy's mom and her brother Philip knew, but that was all. We began to realize that in tragedy, we must know the tension of our pain, or else it would absorb us. Sharing didn't do the trick because Kathy and I, Pamela and Kendall, and Jenn and Gerald were trying to lean on each other, but the pain was cyclical. We kept transferring our crying from one person to the other. We looked at each other but had no words to say. We may have had different ways to express our pain, but it was the same pain. We had lost Miles. Pamela was living in the reminder of losing her baby. The entire family was living in the agony of loss, dealing with yet another death, another time of sorrow and sadness.

We needed to share with someone else. In sharing, you may have an element of clarity, allowing you to think, process, and look at the situation from a different perspective. But interestingly, none of that happened. We thought about what was happening but had no answers. We processed the events before and during, but still, none of it made any sense. We tried to look at it from a different perspective, seeing what God was doing or wondering how others had dealt with a similar event as this, but still, we couldn't see clearly. The tears not only watered our eyes but they blurred our vision. We couldn't function through the tears and the pain. And still, we knew. There was something in us we knew, but what was it we knew?

Battle of the Week

You don't die from a broken heart; you only wish you did.
—Unknown

In Christianity, we observe Holy Week, which focuses on the events of Christ leading up to his eventual death on the cross, his burial, and his resurrection. In that week, Jesus was celebrated on his entrance into the city of Jerusalem, and later in the week, he met with the boos and jeers of the same people who shouted, "Crucify him." In Scripture, we are told how dark it was from noon until his last breath around three (Luke 23:44, Matthew 27:45, Mark 15:33). The skies were described as black, and the surrounding area made it seem as if it were midnight, even though it was midday.

Miles' stillbirth gave me a sense of what it must have been like in those days. I was in a dark place. Daylight would come, but darkness surrounded me. The sun may have been shining, but every second of the day, it felt as if I were in a storm.—a storm without rain and filled with dark, thundering clouds. Hurt, sorrow, and pain will do those things to you. You feel your face smile, but on the inside, you are screaming. You put on the façade of being okay, knowing on the inside you are a mess. I know the agony I was feeling can never compare to the agony of Christ on the cross. But it was my agony and my darkness. It was real. It was agonizing, and it was a living death.

Holy Week is named because of the outcome of Jesus's resurrection and ascension into Heaven. Yet, I can't help but think of his mother, Mary. Mary had reared Jesus. She fed him, bathed him, and loved him. She may have even put him in time-out, although I highly doubt it. She watched him grow in favor of men. Mary was his mother, and she cared for him. And now she had to give him up. She heard the ridicule of the people and watched the excruciating pain of the crucifixion. Her heart was broken, and she had to cry in silence. Was this truly Holy Week or hell week?

I know for us, going through this time, it was hell week. We couldn't see anything holy in what we were experiencing. We didn't see God being in any of this or having a purpose for this. Kathy had a cousin, Julie, who had lost a baby to stillbirth more than twenty years ago. We recalled her loss during our dark time. We remembered the tiny casket and the funeral service Kathy's dad performed, as well as the whispering and the conversations. We remembered how frail and jaundiced Julie looked at the time but didn't recall the enormity of the loss, the pain she went through, or the difficulties she had to endure in being alone at that time.

How many other women have been alone? Jenn had her family around her. Many other women do not. They suffer, like Mary, in the privacy of their hearts. They don't have a support system in place. They don't have anyone to hold them or stand with them. Who is there to help them through or to give them a reason to live again? Kathy has since reached out to Julie to let her know how loved she is and how horrible we felt about not knowing what she was going through back then. We've also had the blessing of finding out several women in our church have had to endure their own hell week, hell years, and in some cases, a lifetime of living in the hell of their own thoughts of guilt, shame, embarrassment, and failure.

Little did we know how widespread it was to lose a child who was born sleeping. As of September 2022, there were an estimated twenty-four to twenty-six thousand stillbirths annually in the United States. Yes, the United States of America is the richest country in the world, with some of the most advanced technology, medical research, and resources in the world. And yet, on average, twenty-five thousand families are devastated every year at the loss of a child born sleeping. Worldwide, the number is upwards of 2.6 million every year. African American and Native American families suffer at a rate four times that of other races and families. Economic status doesn't protect you either, as most stillbirths are in countries with middle-to-high income rates.

The data are available and out there for anyone to research and discover for themselves. But when you are going through it, statistics mean nothing. Information about others living through the horror and pain of such loss does not ease your pain or heartache. Trying to associate with Mary doesn't help much, either. It seems as if, when you are in your own hell week, you cannot see anything else. There is no light, no vision, no hope. Only a dark sky pervades the entirety of your existence. The cloud that hovers over you is like the most intense storm with no rain, just thunder and an eerie sense of doom and dread. It is an endless span of blackness above you. It is a staying-in-your-room, curtains-drawn-shut kind of darkness. No light in, no lights on, no light is anywhere to pierce your teary eyes. This is hell week. Nothing holy, nothing godly, nothing prophetic; only hurt, anger, pain, and sorrow exist. Trying to see, hear, or feel God is nonexistent. All you know is that during that time of loss, it seems as if it will never end.

Not Just Another Day

On the Wednesday of our hell week, Kathy and I made our way to Columbus. Jenn was at the Ohio State University Hospital. They still used pandemic protocols, allowing Jenn only to have two people on her visitor's list. However, with everything going on, God shared his wisdom with us, his favor, and his blessing, so we would know that he was with us. He was in our pain and sorrow, hurt and anger, anguish and confusion, questions and concerns, and our sadness and tears. God was in it all. Just because we couldn't sense him didn't mean he wasn't there. When you are hurt deeply and can't feel, you don't know anything other than what is in front of you. Emotions pour over your head. You don't recognize the signs of God being with you, but then, God pushes through just enough for you to know he is there.

When Jenn was making her list of visitors, Gerald suggested, since she was admitted to the hospital under her married name, she put down Kathy as her other visitor. Her list consisted of Gerald and Kathy. This was so her pastor could come to visit—Pastor Michael Bullock of Hands of Faith Church. So it was that Kathy and I both got to visit Jenn at the same time, at the same moment, to share in the hurt of our little girl together.

We found our way to the maternity ward and gently knocked on the door. Jenn was alone, as Gerald had gone home to tend to Noah and Harper and have a hot shower. It was also his time to find a quiet moment to gather himself. Upon seeing Jenn, a few tears flowed—quiet, gentle tears. The kind of tears that speak to a situation without saying anything out loud. Words were exchanged. "How are you? How are you feeling? What do you need? What can we get you?" What else do you say? We've never been through something like this before and were trying to make it through the moment, get through the day and the pain. We had no other choice. Though we are people of faith, we still didn't know what to say to our little girl.

If You Don't Know What to Say . . .

Sometimes people say things they don't mean, and you just have to let it go.
—Joe Manganiello

In the following months, we discovered some things people say are difficult to take. It's hard because people don't always know what to say in those situations, and quite frankly, sometimes we wish they hadn't said anything at all. We heard from other women who had lost a child or had a miscarriage, and they shared things that were said to them as well. A variety of people, some in ministry, some in our family, and others who were friends, said things that let us know how little they understood the situation.

"Well, she has two other kids she needs to concentrate on."
"When will she be back at work? We miss her on air."
"Everyone loses someone in life; it's just the way it is."
"It was just a baby, not like a child or an adult."
"She can always adopt; there are a lot of kids that need families."

As a pastor, I've learned people may speak without thinking. I can usually move on and let it go. But in full confession, some of these words were met with a retort stemming more from my fatherly anger and less from a pastoral heart. And I didn't apologize. These words were probably my failed attempt to protect my little girl because I had failed at doing so with Miles. I felt justified in lashing out or rebuking the ridiculous comments that had no place at that moment. I am sure some people think it inappropriate for a pastor to act this way, but I wasn't a pastor; I was a daddy. However, I must admit, for a moment, it felt good to speak my mind, say what I felt, and not hold back. Speaking my mind was liberating, even if not politically or socially acceptable or correct.

We've learned a great deal about the human heart and our society's ills when it comes to empathy and understanding someone else's pain. We've become a society numb to others while loudly announcing our own pain and problems. I guess it is why, as a family, we stay private. We stay within ourselves, and we stay in our lane. We just carry on every day, keeping to ourselves, sharing in each other's burdens, and living behind closed doors. But we also understand, as we stood in Jenn's hospital room, there are times you don't know what to say. Sometimes words don't need to be said. They just need to be felt.

Some Moments Aren't Meant to Last

An angel from the Book of Life wrote down my baby's birth.
Then she closed the book and whispered,
"Too beautiful for earth."
—Unknown

As Kathy and I slowly made our way to the chairs in the room, Jenn asked if we wanted to see Miles. It was one of those questions we already had the answer to but didn't want to seem too anxious about. Kathy and I hadn't talked about it to this point, about seeing the baby, about seeing Miles. We weren't sure if it was permissible or if we had the right to ask Jenn. But God, again, opened the doorway and allowed us to walk right through.

The nurse wheeled him in. He was in a little incubator like any other newborn. His white cap covered his head, and a multi-colored patterned blanket covered his little body. The nurse graciously handed him to Jenn, who, with a brief glance, handed him to Nonna. Nonna is Kathy's nickname from the grandkids. They call me Nonno. (It is supposed to be pronounced, "Non-No," but we say, "No-No" because it's what I say to them most of the time, as in "No-no, that belongs to me; don't touch that; get off there; leave that alone," and so on.) Nonna, as it should have been, held him first. Of course, the tears began to flow. She kissed him, cried over him, and held him close to her heart. I'm not sure how long she had him or what she was thinking in her mind. We've never really talked about that part.

On the other hand, watching her, I was getting somewhat nervous. I've never liked holding babies, even our own. It wasn't something I did growing up, nor was it something I felt comfortable doing. I was never a babysitter or someone who handled little kids, so I was a little uncomfortable. I have always been okay with older children because if I dropped them, they could just jump up and run away. But not babies; they thud and then cry, and you get into all kinds of trouble because of it. But it was finally my turn.

He was so tiny, so light, and so small. Miles was seventeen inches long and 3.9 pounds heavy. Even with his cap and blanket, he was so light. I am an observer by nature; it's in my DNA. I looked hard at him. Trying to see the color of his hair, his skin tone, his little fingernails, the wrinkles on his face, and the little nostrils of his nose. his lips had a unique curvature to them and were thin but full. His chin had a small dimple in it, a common trait on Kathy's side of the family. I just held him as a proud Nonno. Even with all my emotions, I wanted him to know I was his Nonno. But then, at that silent and sullen moment, it hit me. Miles was not going to open his eyes and see me, hear my voice, or feel the warmth of my body. Tears began to flow, more than the silent tears but less than the gut-wrenching, heaving kind of tears. Tears I tried to keep off his blanket and his skin, and yet, at the same time, I was hoping my tears would stir something in him that would bring life.

Is Any of This Real?

Life is not a series of meaningless accidents and coincidences.
But rather, it's a tapestry of events that culminates
in an exquisite, sublime plan.
—Unknown

Movies can be misleading to young, impressionable minds. In movies, the prince kisses the girl, and she wakes up from a poisonous sleep. Or the prince cries over the girl, and his tears touch her cheek, and she rises with a smile. Maybe a magic potion touches the lips of the girl, and she wakes up in the arms of her prince charming. Movies and life lie. There is no magic potion, no tears or kisses that can bring someone back to life. Only tears and more tears. Movies and life can be cruel to the mind if you allow them to be seen through jaded eyes.

As I sat holding Miles, I talked to the Lord. Okay, I begged the Lord. I reminded him of his word of truth. *God, whatsoever things we ask, You give them to us, right? God, whoever asks according to your will, you will answer, right? God, whoever has enough faith to speak and believe you do miracles, they will happen, right? God, you used Elijah to bring a little child back to life. You used Elisha to bring someone back to life. You told Ezekiel to speak to a bunch of bones and brought those dry, stinky things back to life. Your Son was walking around, minding his own business, when a father came to him and asked for his child to be brought back to life, and he did it. What about now? What about my grandson, Miles? Please, please, please, I am begging you, let us see a miracle right here, right now. We sing it all the time, how you are a miracle-working God. We read of it in the Bible, all the time, everywhere, how you perform miracles. I am begging you.*

If necessary, take me instead, so my little girl, my wife, and my girl Pamela don't have to live without this little creation of life. I have given you everything I am. I have asked for little, but I am asking for this now: give Miles life, please. Show people your glory and your power. Show them how you transcend time, space, and matter because you are the Creator of all. Let your glory be seen, tangibly, by those who reject you.

God, where are you? Why are you not doing anything? *What is happening right now? I can't breathe; I can't think; I can't see. Where are you? I can't hate you. I won't hate you, but I can be angry with you. And for some dumb, stupid, idiotic reason, even now, I know nothing miraculous is going to happen. You are still God. I know you knew all of this. I know you will someday show us why, but today, this day, I am hurting, my wife is hurting, my son-in-law is hurting, my little girl is hurting, and our family is hurting. Where are you?*

FIVE

Hope for Today and Maybe Tomorrow

Never stop believing in hope because miracles happen every day.

—Karen Salmansohn

H ell week! Jesus had a hell moment in time. I say this only because at the end of his week, there was the resurrection. For one day, he had hell to pay, and then a few days later, he rose again to exhibit the glory of the Father. Don't get me wrong, none of us, not one of us, could have withstood the crucifixion or the punishment of the cross. But in our finite minds, it was still only one day. We, months later, are still living with the pain of the loss of Miles. But then, because of the resurrection, we know at some point, we will breathe and live without the harshness of our pain. Because of what Christ did, we can live knowing there will be a tomorrow. This is what gives Christians hope and allows us to keep living when we experience death and are in the depth of severe pain. We have hope in Christ. We believe strongly and unwaveringly in the resurrection of Jesus Christ. It is why he is our Savior and the one who died for our sins.

If after three days in a tomb, when God raised his Son from the dead, why couldn't he, after three days, raise to life Gerald and Jenn's son, our grandson? Same God, right? Scripture says he is the same yesterday, today, and forever. We are told he is the Lord God and doesn't change. So, why not give Miles back to us? Why not another resurrection that turns our hell week into a holy week?

The painful truth is I still don't have an answer. A few people told us our faith may not have been strong enough. Others asked whether I used anointing oil, as though it were some magic potion that God needed to help him be God. No, I didn't use oil; I used my tears and faith because that's what hurting people do during hell week.

But it was also at that moment I knew God would not answer my plea. At least, not the way I was asking. I knew what he wanted. He didn't want me to keep looking for answers. He wanted me to look for him.

Love Never Fails

Common sense is so rare these days; it should be classified as a superpower.
—Unknown

Men can be real goofballs at times. Hear me out on this. I will call out to Kathy, asking where she is in our home, until I find her and walk to wherever she may be. Of course, she wants to know why I'm screaming like a knucklehead and looking for her. I say it's because I have an important question to ask her: "Did you wash my shirt?" or "Did you see where I left my shoes?" or "Where's the remote?" It's funny how instead of looking for it yourself, you try to find the person who may have the answer for you.

See how that works? God was trying to get me to call out to him. I was looking for answers. I was screaming out to God for some solution. I was yelling at him to find words to put to my lack of understanding. And the reality was, he wanted me to find him.

Jeremiah, the prophet, once wrote, "Call to me, and I will answer you and tell you great and unsearchable things you do not know" (Jer. 33:3). As much as I wanted answers about Miles, God was leading me to the answer, his Son. Not to have my questions supplied with results but for comfort, wisdom, and strength. In him, I would find what I was looking for—peace and comfort in the middle of my hell week.

Scripture tells us of this mysterious happening during Holy Week. During the time of his entombment, it says Jesus descended into hell, or in the Greek word, Hades. It is a state of death explaining how Jesus died. It was not so much about a place as much as it was about recognition of an act we experience as human beings. Because sin entered in, death became a reality. For Jesus, Hades was not a finality or a destination in which he would reside. He resurrected, came back to life after his death, and now lives forevermore.

What God was getting into me at that moment was that Miles' state of death was not his final destination. He was going to be resurrected, *is* resurrected, and is living forevermore. Miles is not living with me or us on this earth. He is in Heaven, waiting for us to get there. This was God's way of trying to get me to understand that for him, as the Father of the greatest Son on earth, he, too, had a hell week that turned into a holy week. Loving Miles is to want the best for him. Where Miles is in Heaven, there is no better place. The pain, the heartache, the longing for his presence, and all the emotions we experienced and still experience are lived out every day.

But love, true biblical agape love, is to want more for the person you love than for yourself. God so *loved* the world that he gave up his Son. Yes, we have a God who understands our sorrows and our hurts. He knows our frustrations and anxieties along with our fears and torment. He knows what it's like to be unable to help those you love. Our God is not a statue, an animal, or some icon we idolize. God is a living Spirit who we worship, even during hell week, until we find that moment when our hell becomes holy. Love does that—God's love, the love he shares with us. He, who *is* love, gave himself for us to experience love on earth. And if we are going to love on earth, then we must deal with the consequences and results of that love: giving up something of ourselves for the betterment of others.

Yes, it stinks and hurts and all those things, but love is a sacrifice and requires an abandonment of self for someone else. Every woman and every family suffering from a stillbirth can rest assured their baby girl or baby boy is in Heaven. I am not concerned with your theology or your religion and do not need to argue aesthetics or preferences of beliefs. I am assured every baby born sleeping is in Heaven. God is love, and in him, there is no hatred. God is merciful and forgiving. He doesn't just love; he *is* love. The purest form of love is a child born sleeping, who is in the arms of a loving heavenly Father.

Tick, Tick, Tick

It is amazing how fast the mind can move. It seemed as if I had been hours sitting in Jenn's hospital room, but it had only been a few minutes. I was having an intense, internal conversation with God, causing me to lose track of time. Truthfully, it really wasn't a conversation. It was a rant. I talked, complained, and told God things I am sure he already knew. But then, what had been a rant slowly turned into a revelation. I talked, and God didn't respond. I won't say he wasn't listening because the Lord hears the prayers of those who are his. He hears the cries and pleas of his children. Most of us, when our kids throw a temper tantrum, we tune them out. The rest of the neighborhood or restaurant may hear, but as parents, we tune them out. We don't respond to them until they have settled down. As I finally settled down, I realized God was not going to perform a miracle. He was not, at least at this moment on this day, going to give us an answer. But then, I knew already. I had an answer, *the Answer*. Not the answer I wanted, but the answer I needed.

I handed Miles to Jenn, and she then gave him to Kathy again, who then gave him to me again for the last time. Even now, those words "for the last time" still sting. As I sit and type this, it is Tuesday, October 11, 2022, exactly one year from when we lost Miles. To know we've gone a year without holding him has been hard. We have pictures of him; I have a screen image of him on my phone. Some days, I can look at the pictures and smile, but on other days, I can't because I am already in pain, and his image causes more pain. Sometimes, I look at his picture to be encouraged about eternity. But in the hospital at OSU that Wednesday, I said goodbye for the final time. Yes, I know it was even harder for Jenn and Gerald. I am not dismissing their loss or their pain. I know it was hard for Kathy and even more so for Noah and Harper, who were expecting a baby brother to come home. I also know it was hard on Pamela, Kendall, and their little boy, Michael, who lost a cousin.

But I can't speak for them and their pain. All I can do is share the pain with you of how I felt and what I was experiencing. A pain and experience that was somewhere along the lines of theirs. To know I would hold Miles for the last time is a statement of finality. Death stings: it stinks; it's unfair, and it is final. Everyone in this life has experienced the death of someone they loved. You hate the fact that death is final in this life. But even in that, as believers, we know there is an eternity, but eternity isn't now. And though the sting of death hurts in this life, it won't hurt in eternity. We feel its effects, and we feel it piercing our hearts. Death creates a gap between Earth and Heaven, and there is nothing more we can do about it. We either learn to live with the loss, or we sink into a pit of despair, not living the life meant for us. Death has a profound effect on us all. But the Christian life is not about death, sorrow, and pain. It is about how we respond to death, sorrow, and pain and how we choose to live each day, moving forward and living by God's grace.

Gerald returned to the hospital room as Jenn was being discharged later that day. Kathy and I went to the grocery store to buy items for their house before joining them there to see what we could do. Or, at least, see what I could do to fix it—I had to *do* something because I didn't have any answers. The problem was, at this point in our journey,

I was tapped out. It was an exhausting feeling that went beyond just being tired, the kind of exhaustion where your mind is at a loss for words. Your heart has no capacity to feel anything but numbness. Your eyes have no tears left, and your vision is less than focused. Your body simply hurts.

Being tapped out is, however, different from tapping out. My brother-in-law loves WWE™ wrestling. I remember years ago watching Bobo Brazil, Andre the Giant, Hulk Hogan, and a few others in the ring. Occasionally, there would be tag team partners: brother duos or big-name wrestlers coming together for a match. Whenever they got into a tight spot in their matches, they would have to get to the side of the ring and tap their partner's hand. They tapped out. They would step outside the ring and let their partner take over. They gave up; they quit, even if it was only for a few minutes. They took a break and sat out. Kathy and I couldn't tap out. We didn't see ourselves taking a break. We didn't allow for a moment's rest or a period of sitting out. Because as hard as things had been up to this point, little did we know it was about to get harder. The days ahead were about to become even more challenging than we could have ever imagined.

SIX

Without Faith, What Do You Have?

It is important for all of us to appreciate where we come from and how that history has really shaped us in ways that we might not understand.

—Justice Sonia Sotomayor

athy grew up in a Christian home. Her father, the Reverend Cecil (Dean) Tabler, was a pastor and preacher. He was a good man with a good heart, and he was gracious to everyone. Her mom, Yvonne, taught Sunday school, helped with the youth, and sang in the choir. Her older brother Tony and younger brother Gregg were in church and youth group, doing what their mom and dad told them to do. Church was everything to them, and they lived it Monday through Saturday, not only on Sundays. They were and still are true believers. Kathy's father and younger brother Gregg have passed on (spending time with Miles already). Her other brother, Philip, is in ministry with us currently. He is an amazing pianist and speaker, and he has several of his dad's tendencies when it comes to caring for people. Church and faith have always been a part of her family's lives.

As for me, on the other hand, religion did not play much of a part, if at all. From birth to twenty-one, I think I graced the church doors no more than six times. At age fourteen, I went to a youth meeting at a church in the community where I went to high school. The preacher asked us to lift our hands if we wanted Jesus. I lifted my hand, but it wasn't for Jesus. It was because the girl I liked at the time lifted hers. I figured it was a good way to get her to be my girlfriend. Apparently, I didn't hear the part about lifting your hand for Jesus; my eyes were on the girl. We were taken into a back room and asked about our *decision*, and I pretty much told them I had no idea what I was doing. Just so you know, the first girl never became my girlfriend.

The next time I was in a church was after I'd met Kathy, and well, I wanted to impress her too. Kathy had made it very clear; I was a sinner, and she was not. She was a churchgoing, faith-filled woman, and I was a frivolous, flirtatious, arrogant man.

Not being a church-going person, the only church I knew to take her to was in Columbus, my hometown. It was a church that several of my relatives attended. Many of my cousins, aunts, and uncles were members of this church. I decided to take Kathy there, thinking I would be safe. Plus, the church was just a few miles from where Kathy attended college at Capital University.

One Sunday morning, off we went. Little did I realize the stir it would create in my family for them to see me in *their* church with this pretty, intelligent, and sweet girl. By their expressions, you would have thought Jesus was coming back that morning. However, within a year, instead of trying to impress Kathy and get her to like me—let alone fall in love with me—God used her to trap me. It was the proverbial raising of the hand to get the girl, but I was the one that got got. God called me into a relationship with him, and then he called me into the ministry a few years later. God got me, and I got the girl. Sometimes, I still think I got the better of the deal.

I share our differences and how we came together because Kathy and I have always (and I don't use that term lightly) lived our lives by faith. She from an upbringing and me from not knowing anything about the Lord to living every day and trusting him with my life. But the problem, sometimes, in Christianity, is that people put their faith in faith. In other words, they put so much value in what they believe was taught to them (or in a tradition passed down) that they forget or never learned how to put their faith in God.

In life and ministry especially, you start to put your faith in your faith. You keep trying to believe what you see and the results of what you are trying to do in leading people, leading a church, or raising a family in the church. You put your faith in your belief that God is going to do this or God is going to do that on your behalf. You do this to feel confident, knowing you are on the right track. It's for his glory, you say, but you want to be rewarded as well. So, you keep putting your faith in your faith, hoping God will reward your efforts to impress him.

The problem with that line of thinking is when your faith is shaken and your world is turned upside down, you double whatever you've put your faith in. You ask the wrong questions, such as, "Why is this happening to us?" "Why would God allow this to happen?" "What is God trying to tell us, teach us, do to us, or show us?" When we're trying to solve life's problems and difficulties, relying on our strength rather than God's, we have faith in faith. We should have faith in God.

Having faith in faith puts my trust in what I do for God and not in who God is. God doesn't have to prove himself to me or anyone else to be God. God doesn't have to *make* people believe he is real for him to be real. There are historical figures I have never met, nor have I seen accurate pictures of them, but in school, we are told they are real, so we believe it. But regarding God, whom no one has ever seen, when people are told he is real, they don't believe it. They think *I can't see him, I can't touch him, and I can't feel him.*

These are all valid statements, but they are not good arguments because I could say the same thing about Abraham Lincoln or Buffalo Bill, yet we know they existed. That's why when you put faith in faith and your faith is shaken, silly questions arise for which you have no rational answer. But when you put your faith in God, the kind of faith that recognizes your lack of understanding in life, you find he is the answer. You find out he is God and forever will be God. This God kind of faith is not shaken, nor does it create unanswerable questions. This is the kind of faith, the raise-your-hand faith, that says, "I came for one thing (to get the girl) and found something else (I got God)." I'm admitting that Miles' stillbirth shook our faith. The faith we had in faith. But it also brought us back to the foundation of what our family is about and what our marriage was built upon—faith in God.

When you have nowhere else to go and nothing else to hold on to, put your faith in God. Don't put your faith in the church, preacher, deacon, or family members. Nor in an alcoholic beverage, a pill bottle, or other drug of choice. Putting your faith in other people, sexual activity, or another numbing experience to escape your darkness or hell week won't work either. Put your faith in God, who will amply supply you with what you need, even if you don't know what that is. Loss is not the same as being *lost*. Don't get lost in a situation where you've experienced a loss. Life can still be lived, and love can still be found. You must find the one who has been looking for you to raise your hand and say, "I need help, and there is nowhere else for me to go but to you, Lord." Maybe you won't get the girl, but you can still get God.

SEVEN

How Dark is Dark?

When everything goes to hell, the people who stand by you
without flinching–they are your family.

—Jim Butcher

We had arrived at Jenn and Gerald's home. On the surface, things seemed to be proceeding well. Pamela and Kendall had brought all the kids to the house, and the whole family was there except Miles. His absence created a void that changed the atmosphere of the house. There was a stirring disrupting the calm and the normalcy of our being together. We were feeling a little uneasy because we faced unfinished business. We knew that telling Noah, Harper, and Michael that their little brother and cousin was not coming home was going to be difficult, and it proved to be more emotional than we had envisioned. How do you explain death and loss to a five-year-old child and a four-year-old and then try to explain it to an almost two-year-old? As Jenn shared the story of what happened, their little eyes fixated on her and her words. Ordinarily, as any parent knows, kids don't listen. Heck, they don't sit still long enough to hear anything you say. But there they all sat. It was surreal to see these little tykes intrinsically engaged in the conversation as if they had reached an adult level of comprehension within a matter of minutes.

Michael, our most inquisitive grandchild, asked many questions. Of course, being five, his questions weren't that deep, and yet, they were: "Jenn, how do you feel? Are you sad? When will we see Miles? Is he with Jesus right now? Did you get to hold him?" Michael's little mind was trying to process it all and get a grip on the situation without fully understanding death and life, loss, grief, and emptiness. Yet, he felt it. He felt what we were feeling, even if it wasn't at the depth of our understanding. But then, we weren't understanding either. What he didn't realize was at the age of five, he was already at the same level as his parents, his Nonno and Nonna—everyone.

How do we feel? What causes such sadness? Why did death have to be so hard, and why is it even a part of life? Quite the irony, death is a part of life. It is interesting how, either as an adult or a child, grief and sorrow link you spiritually together. The level of hurt may be different. But the power of death's impact proves to synchronize your lives. Michael is an amazing little boy, as are all our grandchildren. He stood, staring at Jenn, hanging on to her every word. Finally, he had no more questions and simply stood in silence and bewilderment, wondering, much like the rest of us.

Noah, our little processor, took a different approach. Noah and Michael are eleven months apart. They act more like brothers than cousins, so Noah sometimes feels more like a younger sibling to Michael, even though he is the older brother to Harper. At first, he asked a few questions about Miles. "How big was he? You mean we can't see him? Did you touch him, Mommy? Did Nonna and Nonno see him?" And then, he began to cry. He cried like an adult, the heaving, collapsing, sobbing kind of crying that someone who is deeply affected cries. But how can a four-year-old cry such tears at something even we adults have no understanding of? Gone was his quirky little smile. Gone was his Ninja Turtle and Paw Patrol playtime, as well as his creativity for coloring dinosaurs. And gone was his boyishness because he entered an adult tragedy. Jenn sat and held him, with Michael standing beside her.

Harper looked on in wonder, her innocence still intact. She held on tightly to her favorite pink blankie. Binkie piercing her lips, she sat on Jenn's knee. Three of our four living grandchildren. (K'Niyah, our son-in-law Kendall's daughter, was away. She is loved and as much a part of our family and journey.) They stood and sat with Jenn, occupying her space as if to try to fill the void left behind by Miles. They cried, they stared, and they asked questions. Still, their pain remained. The tears on their faces and the image of them with Jenn are forever seared in my mind. Jenn was trying to put aside her own pain, tears, heartache, and sorrow to attend to her children and her nephew.

Somehow, I thought it was going to be okay and we would get through this. The deep sorrow lasted for several more minutes. But then, as kids do, without fanfare, Noah was off the couch and gone. Michael ducked behind the couch to play with his dinosaurs. Harper sat in Nonna's lap, still trying to understand what was happening. We all sat and chatted for a few more minutes, rehashing what had just transpired and still trying to make sense of it all. It was then we realized we hadn't seen Noah. Getting concerned, I got off the sofa to see where he had gone. Now, mind you, this was mid-October, and Halloween festivities were a few weeks away. The kids had their costumes already picked out and were getting excited about their first memorable candy collection.

Suddenly, out of his room, Noah emerged in his Flash costume and zipped around the living room, into the kitchen, past the dining room, and back into his bedroom. After several more trips around the house, Noah returned to being a kid again. We laughed, not the kind of gut-touching laugh, but more along the lines of needing to experience something resembling the opposite of crying.

Laughter is good. Wouldn't it be cool if, as adults, we could put on costumes to escape our reality? Wouldn't it be fun to run around in our undies and play with dinosaurs while holding our favorite blanket? Yes, we were going to be okay. Little did I know this was the calm before the storm. I wasn't reading the atmosphere of the room. There was no radar telling me there was danger ahead and that life would continue to change. We were about to experience unexpected darkness and grief, loss, trauma, despair, depression, and mental anguish that we didn't see coming. An emotional roller coaster we didn't know existed in people who loved Jesus was about to take off from the platform.

When the Lights Are Out

Kathy went into the kitchen to prepare dinner for all of us. Pamela tended to the kids and their needs. Kendall left to do some work. I began picking up clothes and toys and doing anything I could to continue trying to fix the situation. Gerald led Jenn back into the bedroom, or what I would later call the abyss.

I've had moments in life that have been dark and bleak when I felt life wasn't worth living—times when I hated people, hated myself, and hated being alive. But mostly, they were passing thoughts, depressing thoughts, and thoughts eventually passing with time.

In the Boomer Generation, of which I am a member, mental health and abuse issues weren't talked about. Back then, they weren't even subjects to be discussed. But today, in our culture and society, with the advancement of the psychiatric and psychological fields, we know more about the human brain and how it works. We also have a greater sense of the emotional trauma people go through. I am not sure when the switch flipped, and we went from non-discussion to full-blown discussion, but we have put words to how we feel and what we deal with.

Jenn was in a dark place. She was in a place where she desired to be. She wanted to be more with Miles than the rest of us. Kathy would go in and lay on the bed with her, hold her, and cry with her. She would sit with her, trying to get her to eat, get up, bathe, move, or do something. But nothing changed. When Kathy would wear down, she would call for reinforcements, which would be me. I would go in and pray with Jenn. I would sit with her and hold her as her daddy and not as her pastor. At one point, I just kept saying how proud of her I was, but I'm pretty sure she didn't hear a thing I said. One afternoon, she asked me, "Daddy, why did God do this?"

For those of you who don't know, I completed a degree in Business Management, a Scofield Biblical Studies Certification, a master's degree from Moody Bible Institute, and earned my doctorate from Regent University. I've learned from books, conferences, post-graduate classes, and conversations with brilliant individuals. I have done my due diligence to hone my craft and present a better version of myself over time. But at that moment, my little girl asked me, "Daddy, why did God do this?" My theologically intense training and years of experience garnered one response; "Baby, I don't know." How un-profound and stupid. A lot of good all the years of training and learning did me.

Jenn stayed in her room, in her abyss. She was in a deep, dark place, not knowing if or when she would hit bottom. Her mom would come in. I would come in. We would tag-team, doing whatever we could. We found out what big-time wrestlers knew: you need a break, a rest, so you step out of the ring. It wasn't quitting; it was refueling. I needed a partner to help me hang in there. Kathy needed a partner to help her hang in there. We needed each other because Jenn needed the best from each of us.

Our tag-team efforts went on for a few days. I had cleared as much of my schedule as I could. I tried to maintain a normal regimen and schedule. I still had sermon preparation to tend to and church duties and responsibilities. Kathy took a week of vacation to drive back and forth from Columbus to Zanesville and from Zanesville to Columbus. She and I would do so every day, from early in the morning until late at night, praying and crying before God for our little girl.

In the solitude of my car, I found myself asking God questions. *How do I help my baby girl get out of this? How do I make sense of this? And, Lord, why did you do this?* Maybe if he answered me, I could give Jenn an answer. As much as we tried to help, do, and perform, Jenn stayed in her room, in bed—her dark place, in what resembled an abyss. Kathy would pray, I would pray, and we would pray together, and still, we saw no movement, no life, and no activity from Jenn.

I must admit, the most challenging thing for someone who's been in a dark place is to think positive thoughts about difficult situations. All I could think about during this week was how I couldn't lose both Miles and my little girl. I wouldn't be able to handle it. I was starting to lose it and didn't know what else to do or where to turn for help. I had been praying, begging again for God to intervene, to show himself, to *prove* to me that he truly is God and is real.

Relentless Pursuit

During this entire time, Kathy busied herself at Jenn's home. She did what moms always do. She mopped, swept, dusted, fixed food, washed laundry, and anything she could do. The other thing she did was keep talking to Jenn. She would talk to her, pray with her, and simply be with her. She was relentlessly loving her daughter. She wasn't going to give in or give up on Jenn, and she wasn't going to allow her to stay in the abyss. At one point, Jenn even asked Kathy, "Mom, you're not going to quit bugging me, are you?"

Looking back on that moment, it sounds humorous. But it was necessary. Kathy wanted Jenn to know she wouldn't leave her. Kathy somehow knew Jenn felt God had left her and let her down. Miles had left her, and now Jenn felt alone. But as her mother, Kathy wasn't going to leave her or let her down. Not all women have that instinct within them. Not all women will give everything to their children. But there are those women, like my wife, who will give everything all the time to benefit their children.

It is a God thing. What Kathy was doing is the same thing God does with us. We may not always know it or feel it, but he is relentless in his pursuit of us. He is constant in tracking us down and pursuing us to have an eternal relationship.

We may not always see him or feel him to know he is there. But he is. God's presence through his Spirit is always after us. It is the concept of King David's words. David shared how God's goodness and love follow and pursue us all the days of our lives (Psalm 23:6). God doesn't leave us or let us down. He just doesn't. It's not in his nature. He knows nothing else other than to keep after us until we find him. He pushes us, if you will, out of the darkness and into his light. It is God's relentless love that finds us. Then we find him. We love because he first loved us (1 John 4:7-8).

God's love changes everything for us. When we can't feel God, and when we are in those deep, dark, abysmal places in life, God sends moms. Or he may send fathers, preachers, friends, or counselors. He may send anyone who will be relentless in getting us out of the environment that has swallowed us up.

Leaving Is Not an Option

Never stop doing little things for others. Sometimes those little things occupy the biggest part of their hearts.
—Unknown

Several days after losing Miles, Kathy was leaving our church sanctuary when a hand gently grabbed her. It was one of our younger women who asked for a moment. She shared with Kathy about her having a stillbirth several years ago. She spoke of what she went through and talked about her tears and pain. But it was her last few words Kathy gravitated to. She said, "Don't give up on Jenn. Don't stop going after her. Don't quit on her. Don't stop talking to her." These were all the words Kathy needed to keep pursuing

Jenn. Words that spoke to her about being consistent and relentless, telling her not to give in to her own fatigue. Words to encourage her and urge her to ignore her own pain.

If you know someone in a dark place, in a desperate situation, or someone struggling to find joy, go after them. Stay with them. Be relentless. It is the best way you can love them. Your relentless love lets them know they are loved. And relentless love is God-like love.

It's easy to serve God when things are going well. What do you do when things don't go well? In the direst of situations, both a believer and an unbeliever will turn to people of faith and request prayer. They look for hope and long for relief. Christians desire to hear from God. They hunger for answers. I have believed in God and his Son, Jesus Christ. I have done so since the age of twenty-one. I have known myriad things during my relationship with him. I knew when he called me to preach. Kathy and I knew when it was time to start our church. I knew when he would tell me to keep going when I wanted to quit.

But in this moment of my life, I received nothing—no words, no speaking, no new perspective from any heavenly being. As the saying goes, nothing but crickets. No inspirational words or movements came from the Spirit. No prophetic utterances, signs, wonders, or miracles, only dead, dull, denying silence. It is amazing how God speaks to us when He's not speaking to us.

While awaiting death on the cross, Jesus uttered words that broke the silence of the situation. He begged the Father by saying, "My God, my God, why have you forsaken me?" Those words resonated with me—it was as if they were my own. Often, we can read something, we can teach it, preach it, and even share it with others. But for the first time in all my years of serving Christ, I finally felt those words. *God, my God, why have you done this to us? Why is this happening? Where are you? Why are you not speaking? Why are you not moving? Why are you not doing anything? Why have you forsaken us?* I asked these repetitive questions and others. I asked, and I asked him for weeks.

And then the silence began to break—that deep-seated, sickening feeling of complete isolation from God. After all the preceding events that had caused me to collapse physically, emotionally, and mentally, it was finally happening. Things were beginning to shift. I was feeling an element of strength in me again. It wasn't what anyone was saying through prophetic words. Nor was there an earth-moving experience. There was no shining light from the sky. It was one powerfully moving event leading to the beginning of my breakthrough. Our hell week was turning into Holy Week. Our faith in faith was once again being restored to our faith in God. Though Miles was not resurrected before our eyes, there was a resurrection taking place. Jenn, our little girl, the one in the abyss and darkness, the one who had suffered an unmeasurable loss, had found her way out of bed on this fall afternoon.

I don't have a clue what it was like for Mary at the tomb of Jesus. Did she have a revelation she was holding the King of glory, the Son of God, in his resurrected body? I'm not sure what Mary felt and sensed as she touched Jesus. But I do know, and have burned into my mind's eye, the image of Jenn getting out of bed. Watching the wonderful scene of her being led by Kathy to go take a bath. I breathed in such a manner I could literally feel the air fill my lungs. For the first time in days, I was breathing freely, without tension. Kathy had tears in her eyes. Noah and Harper let everyone in the house know that Mommy is taking a bath. Noah jumped up and down and shouted. "Yeah, Mommy!"

It's amazing how kids are. In her bedridden state, Noah would intermittently go into her bedroom. He would stand at Jenn's bedside and simply say, "I miss you, Mommy." It's funny, not in a comical sort of way, how the insights of children can lead adults. We don't think they even comprehend what is happening. Noah somehow knew Jenn was there physically but was absent emotionally and mentally.

In her own words, Jenn never left us spiritually or physically. Neither did she leave God spiritually, but she left everything else. She left emotionally and mentally. She left her husband, Gerald. And though she loves him, needs him, and leans on him, in her state of sorrow, she still left him. She left him, knowing Noah and Harper were in good hands. She trusted Gerald to take care of them, her home, and her affairs and to answer the calls of her co-workers and friends. She had checked out mentally and emotionally to find her baby boy Miles in some spiritual capacity. She wanted to try to make sense of it all, to try to figure out what she could have done differently.

She left Gerald to find answers as to what the doctors could have done sooner. Answers that maybe could have made this horrible nightmare go away. A nightmare she didn't want to turn into a lifelong aching in her heart. She left Noah and Harper only for a few moments. She left them in the hands of Gerald and her mommy, Kathy. She knew they would be okay because both Gerald and Nonna would take care of them. Even Nonno was able to do some things at times. She also knew if things got tight, Pamela was always there—always, not just once-in-awhile or when it was convenient, but always there.

Jenn could leave every element of mental torment and emotional strain behind. She could leave to try to find Miles in a thought, a memory, or possibly in a feeling within her womb. She would leave us emotionally and mentally, trying to get closer to Miles or at least find a space where she could hold him while trying to hold on to the rest of us. But then, finally, she realized she couldn't stay gone and leave us indefinitely. She couldn't leave Gerald, Noah, or Harper. She knew, instinctively, what believers know: we cannot leave until it is our time to leave.

Jenn agreed to eat some fries and have a Coke™. She got out of bed and came back to us. Her mom helped her into the bathtub. As her daddy, the fixer guy, I went to McDonald's™ and got those fries and a Coke. It was my small gesture to help fix it for my little girl. If you hang around our family long enough, you'll learn fries and a Coke fix emotional setbacks. She was up, bathed, fed, and for a solitary moment, she cracked a smile. She transitioned from the bathroom to the living room, giving us further joy as she continued moving. Bracketed by Noah and Harper on the couch, she smiled. Not a fake grin or some resemblance of lips being parsed, but a real smile, a genuine, tooth-sharing smile. It wasn't a denial of her sorrow or pain. They were still there and very present. Rather, it was a recognition that she had hope again—life was going to go on for her. In this resurrection moment, she was choosing to live in her pain and grief. She knew she could no longer leave us emotionally, mentally, spiritually, or (God forbid) physically. As much as she wanted to leave and be with Miles, she knew she had to live. It is the deep, God-inspiring soul that finds its faith in God. Jenn had found this resource and knew she had to live.

We all sat around the living room. We were having a hallelujah moment, embracing the resurrection of our daughter. And even if we could not see the resurrection of Miles, we knew he had been resurrected. There they both were. One resurrected into the bosom of Christ; the other resurrected into the arms of her loving family. One spiritual, the other physical. Both a delight and joy of knowing our faith in God was growing stronger. We were finding our way to another level of belief. We were finding our way to hope and finding joy once again as a family.

A phrase amongst church people says something like, "Hold on, 'cause Sunday's coming." Which means resurrection day, a day of joy, is on its way. Because everything had happened so quickly and abruptly, life around us kept moving. No matter how badly we wanted it to stop, it kept going. Work was still being done. Bills still needed to be paid. Groceries had to be purchased. Clothes needed cleaning. And sermons still had to be prepared for Sunday mornings.

The year 2021 was coming to an end. Christmas that year was okay. Not only was it a little numbing because of Miles, but every Christmas is a reminder of my brother Chuckie. He passed away on Christmas Day. The kids, of course, had a blast, and my wife, as usual, went overboard with the gifts. But that's what moms do. They spoil, supply, and tend to the needs of their children. And as a wise husband, I step aside and let her. I may at times disagree under my breath, but I watch her do what she does best: love our family. Though Christmas was good, we were looking forward to the calendar changing. The year 2022 couldn't get here fast enough. Those past three months were rough. A fresh start would be good for us all.

EIGHT

Time of Transition

*In any given moment we have two options: to step forward
into growth or to step back into safety.*

—Abraham Maslow

Christmas was over, and it was now 2022. This was the
year God's prophetic voice spoke about our church
theme for the year: *The Tide Is Turning in Our Favor.*
I wasn't sure what it meant or how it would look. I just
knew it didn't seem to be a possibility in our immediate
future. Onward we went, and onward we believed, not in
our faith, but in our faith in God. Easter Sunday of 2022
was in April—April seventeenth, to be exact. The reason
this Easter was different, at least for me, was that it became
a time of revelation, an ah-ha moment. A moment of
inspiration and clarity when, for me, the tide would turn.

A time when the wheels of inspiration started spinning, and ideas for this book began to flood my spirit.

As with most preachers and churches, Easter presents an opportunity to share the love of Jesus and share messages revolving around one of several topics of significance. Messages about his life on earth. His time leading to the cross. His death on the cross. And his entombment. What I wanted to talk about this Easter was his resurrection. For those who often wonder how do preachers get their messages? Some use previously written materials. Some teach individual Bible chapters. Others may use life lessons. And like other pastors, I've tried to allow the Holy Spirit to lead and inspire me.

This season, I was led to the book of John. More specifically, the book of John, chapter 11. It is the chapter identifying Jesus as the Resurrection of life. It tells the story of Lazarus's death and his eventual resurrection. If you are not familiar with the story, in previous chapters, we see Jesus befriending the family of Lazarus and his two sisters, Mary and Martha. Jesus is in a different city when word gets to him that his friend, Lazarus, was sick. In classic Jesus-speak, he says the sickness was not something Lazarus would die from. But as the events and days ahead would unfold, Lazarus's resurrection would be to glorify God. Though Jesus spoke these words, the audience of the day did not comprehend them. Lazarus was sick. And there was a story to be told and a truth to be learned. There was also a reality to be confronted.

Lazarus *did* die. And not only did he die, but by the time Jesus showed up, he had been dead for four days. Was Jesus misinformed? Did he make a mistake? Did he miscalculate the time it took for him to travel from one city to another? He's Jesus, so why would he say such a thing if it were not true? And, what took him so long, anyway? How fast did he walk? Did he ride a donkey? Did he ride on a chariot? Where was he?

These are not questions you will read in the Bible. But when you suffer loss, when you've gone through a tragedy or something that alters your life, you have questions. Where are you in this God? Why did this have to happen? What is the purpose, the point, and why must we have so much pain? How long will this pain last, and will it go any deeper? When will I breathe again, and when will I find laughter? To every event and every downward scenario in life, you have questions. We ask soul-searching, self-examining, strength-sapping questions of God. However, he may or may not speak to you and answer your questions when you ask him. And when he does answer, it may not be the way we desire him to.

Redirected Approach

As I continued to re-read the verses I had read so many times, I just couldn't settle on how to approach this Easter sermon. So many thoughts flooded my mind, and at the same time, I continued to raise so many questions continued. I couldn't focus my attention on Jesus the Resurrector. Instead, my focus was on Mary and Martha, the grieving sisters; specifically, the conversation between Jesus and Martha caught my eye and brought the revelation, causing me to redirect my sermon. And more importantly, it caused me to redirect my life in this season.

The words Martha spoke made an eternal impact on me. Her approach to Jesus, her statements, and her sentiment all hit me hard. Have you ever read a book or heard a song creating enthusiasm for you? Have you ever experienced a shift in attitude because of a profound effect someone had on you? When Jesus and Martha engaged in conversation, I saw myself in Martha's shoes. Her words, actions, and assumed emotions were all real to me. Everything Martha did jumped off the pages of my Bible and went directly to my heart. Healing and comfort came through Martha's words. Her time with Jesus was precious. I continue to learn time with Jesus is precious. Time with family and friends is precious. Time, in general, is precious. And as Jesus showed, timing is everything.

A New Day and a New Way

When Jesus entered the town, everyone knew it. He didn't need a social-media grapevine for his notoriety to spread. Mary sat in the house with family and friends, grieving and doing what those who have lost do. Mary was the sister we would, in our current culture, call passive. She is the sister who sat listening to Jesus when he visited. She was the soft-spoken socialite everyone spent time with. If she were a guy, Mary would have been known as a lover and not a fighter. Martha, on the other hand, was the doer and busy one. It was Martha who cleaned, cooked, and lived much of her time in isolation. Yet, she was the sister who went out to meet Jesus.

It was in reading those words for the umpteenth time that I was struck by the epiphany from the words leaping off the page. *Martha went out to meet Jesus.* She didn't wait for Jesus to come to her. She didn't wait for him to come to the house and meet her needs. As a matter of fact, we aren't even told if Jesus was coming for Martha or Mary. Before he showed up, he said, "Let us go to him" (John 11:15). I read the words again. And then I read them one more time. *Martha went out to meet Jesus.* But Jesus was coming to see his friend Lazarus. Scripture said nothing about the sisters. Jesus and his entourage were coming for Lazarus. But Lazarus was dead. Jesus knew he was dead. Why, then, did he dismiss the grieving sisters? Why wouldn't he tend to the needs of the living? Didn't he, at one point, even tell his disciples to let the dead bury the dead (Matthew 8:22)? And *if* he is the Resurrector, and Lazarus had been dead for four days, what's the hurry? Dead is dead, and if Jesus were going to change that, he could do it at any time. Why seemingly dismiss Martha and make her come to him? We are told Martha, as *soon* as she heard Jesus was coming, went to meet him. She was in a hurry. She immediately went out to Jesus. Why? We are not told. But I can understand her anxiousness. She went to meet Jesus, and she was loaded for bear.

In my mind's eye, I have this image of her walking briskly, her brow furrowed, her lips taut, and her face stern. This is not in Scripture, but can you picture it? If you and I were looking for answers to our pain, wouldn't we be in a hurry? And wouldn't we be storming toward the person we felt caused our dilemma in the first place? Martha wanted answers. She wanted to know where Jesus had been and why it took him so long to get there. I understood Martha's feelings. I could relate to the sternness of her face and the intensity visible on her forehead. In moments of questions and anger, your facial expressions alter. The aching and throbbing of your internal organs cause your external extremities to function at a different level, a level of tension unlike any other under normal circumstances. In times of emotional upheaval, you don't see the possibility of learning lessons. Not the kind of tough lessons you don't want to repeat or relive, but lessons that help you. They are the kind of lessons helping you for the benefit of helping others in their time of need. It was Martha's approach to Jesus that helped me see things differently. Martha helped redirect my frustration and distorted perspective. Martha helped me recognize I had much to learn when it came to grief, sorrow, and sadness.

Lessons for Life

Life taught me love is risky.
Death taught me to love even more.
—Maxime Lagacé

The first lesson I had to learn about grieving situations and loss is you want answers. When a person dies, especially unexpectedly, human nature and instinct take over, and we want to know why or how? We ask the doctor or an expert what the cause was, what could have prevented it, or what could have been done differently. When we were able to talk to Jenn after Miles' stillbirth, it was the un-knowing that continued to haunt us. It is what delayed our moving forward. There were a few answers, but they didn't give us the answers we needed. The kind of answer we needed in trying to solve the ever-aching question of why. The kind of answer which would soothe our conscience and ease our pain. Why do these things happen, and why does it hurt so badly? Why were there not more signals, or why wasn't something detected during Jenn's routine doctor visits?

The second lesson I had to learn was that everyone handles loss, death, grief, and pain differently. In the latter part of John 11, we see Mary, like Martha, eventually went out to greet Jesus. Mary had been sitting in their home. Friends and family surrounded her and consoled her at the loss of her brother. In a quiet tone, Martha informed Mary Jesus was outside of their city. Mary, hearing this, rose from her chair and proceeded to find him. Those in attendance thought she was going to the tomb to continue in her mourning. Little did they know she was going out to meet Jesus. Martha went alone to see Jesus. Mary was with a group. Martha had been attending to the chores of the home. Mary was attending to their guests. Now, like Martha, Mary was headed out, at a different time, to see Jesus. But, unlike Martha, Mary fell at the feet of Jesus. Her reaction and response triggered something in Jesus, causing him to groan and be troubled, or more clearly, he was moved in his soul and his spirit. Martha wept alone. Mary wept with her friends. We read Jesus was moved in his spirit (and eventually wept as well). The three grieve the loss of a brother and a friend. They are caught up in sorrow, weeping in a way we can all relate to. They were together and yet separate. As our family or your family, you cry together, but you cry differently. You laugh, you hug, and you share memories together, but differently. I was learning the lesson through Miles and our family. Everyone grieves in a manner suited to their personality and one that fits their character. Some need private moments to be alone in their thoughts and search for answerless questions. They then must delve deep into their thoughts to come to grips with learning how to live with the unknown. Martha's kind of grief means grieving alone, in seclusion, even if you are in a public setting. Others may think you are disengaged, not realizing you are grieving deep down in your soul. Martha's grief is private grief.

Second, some individuals need the support of others. They need others to share their story, pain, and sorrow. They need others to only comfort them and empathize with them because they don't do well alone. Martha needed her time alone, but Mary needed her people—sisters who had different needs, different personalities, and different characteristics. Mary's kind of grief needs friends and supporters. Yes, sometimes misery does love company. Mary had family, friends, coworkers, associates, neighbors, and community leaders around her. She had an army of many to help soothe her pain but didn't want to grieve alone. Mary's grief is community grief. It gathers others around you to help you make it through. It is a public grief played out in public. Everyone knows you are grieving, and they join in. Mary's grief involves the engagement of others.

Third, we see those who grieve like Christ, who moan or are troubled internally. They can be in a crowd of people yet not let on as to what is troubling them until, finally, their grief comes out. Jesus saw Martha, had a conversation, and moved on. Jesus saw Mary, had a conversation, and went to the cemetery. But at the moment he saw the grave, his emotions flowed over. When Martha is alone, we read of no emotion. Mary, being alone, we read of no emotion. We are told Jesus was hurting on the inside, even if he seemed to have it all together on the outside. There are many people like this. But more than most, pastors are a lot like this. We must hold it together for the families, for the grieving, and for those who are hurting. We must be stoic about our exteriors, even though we are torn up in the interior with emotions. Fathers are like that too. Moms cry with their babies. But dads must be hardcore, or so we've been taught. We stand strong and firm on the outside while feeling ripped apart in our inner man. We are more fragile than we let on, but now in our actions, we must remain strong—press on for the family. Every day, we live in our quiet torment until finally, one day, the emotions flood over, and the tears begin to flow, sometimes in public, but mostly in private. This is Jesus's kind of grief. The kind of grief our family knew all too well.

No matter what type of grief you endure, we all grieve, everyone at some point, all of us in humanity. Of all the things in life, grief is the least segregated or prejudicial part of life. It cares nothing about race or ethnicity, doesn't have a political slant, nor does it care anything about status, gender, or intelligence. Grief just hits us all. And it hits hard, below the belt, and in any way it wants to. The worst thing any of us can do is try to make others grieve the way we grieve. We want them to feel better and do it sooner rather than later because it keeps us from feeling their pain and coming to grips with our own. Not only do we not like to grieve, but we also don't like looking into the face of others who are grieving. It is a reminder of our pain. It reminds us of our loss, our suffering, and our time of heartache.

Maybe that's why Jesus desired to keep walking and not stop and spend time with Martha. Yes, he is, was, and always will be Jesus. He is God incarnate. But he was also the Son of Man. Human in all aspects, tempted and tormented like the rest of us. He had raised others from the dead already and healed the sick, blind, lame, and lost. But now, he was confronted with a personal loss. This was an emotional experience he had not gone through.

Think for a moment, how often do we hear of the loss of someone we don't really know? It gives us pause for a minute, but then we move on. Or when we hear of a loss a friend of ours has had to endure, we may send cards, flowers, text messages, and well-wishes, but after a day or two, we've moved on. Looking into the face of someone else's pain and loss is different from when we look in the mirror and see our own. I can escape their hurt or pain, begin to think of life differently and get on with my life. But when death is personal, we react differently. When death is in our faces and at our families' doorsteps, that is what rocks our world. Now, suddenly, we go from looking into the faces of others to others looking at our face, and it is they who want to walk away from us, as we did from them.

But in the end, we must face our hurt and loss. We don't want anyone to tell us how to grieve or how long to live in pain. No advice or counseling. We just want to be allowed to grieve and find answers to our questions. Grief, like the ocean, keeps coming in waves. When we think we can make it, another wave of emotion rolls in. It doesn't stop until, one day, it does. The residue of grief is always with us; we just stop crying so much and so often.

Martha, in her hurried condition, in her grief-stricken agony, confronts Jesus. Whether Jesus was going to pass by her or not, Scripture doesn't tell us. But Martha was going to make sure that not only was he not going to pass by and walk away, but he was going to have to speak to her and look her in the face.

When Grief Challenges Good

The mystery of history is an insoluble problem.
—Henry Ward Beecher

Not being physically present in a past situation challenges you to know what really happened. Whenever we read a book, novel, email, or text message, we usually read according to how we feel or how we would respond. We don't know what Martha's actual tone of voice sounded like, and in the original text of the New Testament, we are not given the intensity of what she said to Jesus.

What we do know, however, is that she spoke first. She broke the ice and made sure there would be a conversation. This gives us a subtle insight into what her mood may have been and how she may have been feeling. First, because she, as a woman, spoke to Jesus before he spoke, she broke cultural protocol. This was not acceptable during this era. Even if she was familiar with Jesus, women didn't carry the same level of respect then as they do now. Women were lowly and uninvolved with men when it came to tradition and funeral arrangements. In life or death, men handled it all, and Martha speaking first was not typical.

Second, as a woman, she spoke to a man. She singled out Jesus and engaged in conversation alone with him. She confronted him and addressed him in her approach. When Jesus sat with the woman at the well, it was because he initiated the encounter and started the conversation, even though it was socially and politically unacceptable. But, in this situation, Martha reversed the process. She approached Jesus, confronted him, conversed with him, getting to him before he could get away, and doing so at a time when it was not acceptable.

Then third, as a lowly woman, she spoke to the Messiah. When Mary saw him, she fell to his feet. She humbled herself, took her lowly position before speaking, and made sure she honored him as the Messiah, the King of kings and Lord of lords. Martha, on the other hand, just stood there, in his face, full of questions and wanting answers. If you have ever been in a deep place of hurt, then you can better understand Martha in this situation. How many times have I said something or done something out of character because my emotions got the best of me? How many times have I acted out my pain, yelling at someone or saying something less than complimentary because I hurt so much and didn't know how else to act? Or how often have any of us done something we regretted and wished we hadn't done? How often have we excused our actions by referring to not knowing what we were thinking or why we did what we did because we were grieving? It is human nature for us to respond to tragedies in a manner unbecoming of what we normally do. It is in our humanity and the grip of grief that we do the unconventional and untraditional because grief creates that kind of effect on us.

When my brother Chuckie died, a family member said things to Kathy as an attack and could have been taken as mean-spirited. Was what was said a reflection of how the person really felt all along about Kathy? Or was it in the pain of the moment? Did the family member feel comfortable saying whatever they wanted to? Was it because they knew my wife, in her sweet disposition and spirit, could handle the reaction at that moment, in that situation, at that time? To this day, I don't know. But what I can say is that it changed how I looked at that person, even to this day. It showed me what grief can do and how pain can expose the depth of our hurt, as well as give insight into a person's character.

Grief challenges us.

Grief changes us.

Grief takes the best people and exposes the worst parts of them at times.

Grief will take good people and cause them to act badly.

Grief challenges everything that is good because death itself is bad.

What we once enjoyed and deeply loved we can never lose,
for all that we love deeply becomes a part of us.
—Helen Keller

NINE

Name Calling

The name of a person you love is more than language.

—Tennessee Williams

My life has been filled with a variety of opportunities in which I've been involved. I have different titles because of this variety of activities. In an academic environment and political circles, I may be referred to as Dr. Bullock (or Dr. B by students). I spent close to twenty-five years coaching high school athletics, so to this day, for many athletes and their parents, I am still "Coach." With our church family and others in the body of Christ, I may be called "Pastor Mike." And in my home, I'm "Hon" (only Kathy calls me this), "Daddy" (to my two girls), "Mr. B" (to my two sons-in-law), and "Nonno" (to my grandchildren). These titles give me a feeling of warmth and familiarity. Depending on which title I am called, I know the environment I am in, and I know the people who call me those things know me, and I know our history together. To the public, however, if I hear, "Mr. Bullock," I know you may know of me or at least respect me, but we are acquaintances. But if you call me "Reverend Bullock," you may know of me with that title, but it says you don't really know me at all. I don't like being called by that title, even if you meant no disrespect. It is in the titles that I know you and our association. Some titles are endearing, while others are complimentary, but they all identify our relationship and connection.

When Martha saw Jesus, she didn't call him by the name she would have been familiar with; she called him "Lord." In the Hebrew language, it is *Adonai*. In the Greek language, it is *Kurios*, which has several meanings to it.

First, it is known as a friendly greeting, such as "sir." Second, it is used in addressing someone who is in a higher position or carries a significant amount of importance by addressing them as *master or owner*. And third, it can be used as a wife addresses her husband. I don't believe this is the context being used because Martha addresses Jesus as Lord. So, we can rule out the husband option. We can, in some manner, rule out her calling him sir, not because he wasn't a man or worthy of the title, but because he was her friend. And she would not have addressed him with a title that was unfamiliar. This leaves us with the title, master. In the Old Testament, whenever we see the word Lord spelled with a capital L and lower-case letters that follow, it leads us to the translation of God as master, owner, supreme in his nature.

Master is also a designation of the relationship the Creator has with creation. God, the Creator, can transcend time, space, or matter. When we address him as Lord, it is because we have a relationship with him, and we know he can do anything he wants to do. He can turn water into wine, cleanse leprosy, or cast out demons. He can walk on the water or tell it to calm down. He can feed thousands with little and take a few things and make much of them. As Lord, he doesn't operate on the same playing field as the rest of us.

Martha knew this firsthand. She knew he was a healer, deliverer, miracle worker, and the One who could resurrect the dead. She didn't need a husband or a neighborhood friend; Martha needed the Creator to intercede for her. She needed the One in whom she had placed her faith. She needed Jesus, the Lord, not the One who is the Son of Man. In essence, she was saying, "Jesus, get out of your flesh and once again be my Lord. My faith right now is shaken, and my faith right now is very fragile. I believe in You, and I know You. You can do anything. Let's get to the tomb and move on from this pain." Martha's faith was shaken. She questioned, wondered, was fragile, and more than anything else, she was being real. Just seeing Jesus, the Lord, opened her heart to the deeper question of how profound and strong your faith is during tragedy.

Faith Is Everywhere

> *Every day in so many ways, God does speak to his children.*
> *Those who know His voice, hear him well.*
> —Gift Gugu Mona

In 1991, God spoke to Kathy and me intuitively. We were in our car, traveling back to Zanesville one evening from Columbus, and in our hearts and our spirits, we both knew God was calling us to start a church. It was a surreal moment. We just knew. I can't tell you how or give you specifics of how God speaks or gives promptings to us, but we knew. There was no doubt and no question. The details at that point weren't clear; we just knew it was him who spoke to us individually, even though everything we shared together was as a team. It wasn't until months later that our church would get started. In our first Sunday morning service in September of 1991, we met with a few dozen good, gracious people who attended the church with no name. Yep, you read that right. At our first church service, we met in a garage and had no name. We just met, put our faith and trust in God's word, and had a church service. The following Sunday, in the evening, we got together with those same morning folks and came up with a name—Hands of Faith Church.

Every minute from then to now, Kathy and I, along with our girls, have tried to live our lives by faith. We have lived by trusting in what God, through Christ, has always said for us to do. Our church started by faith and continues to exist every day by faith. We are people of immense conviction, trusting the Lord for everything we have, and for those things, he decides we either do or do not need. We have always thought we were solid in our faith. But we have had several events which made us question our faith on the surface.

Miles' stillbirth shook our faith, and it also rocked our world. Only in conversation have I come to learn how it rocked all of us. Kathy, the Christian girl from birth, was rocked. My girls, who have always known church and came to Christ and accepted him on their own, too, were rocked. Jenn, more understandably than the rest of us, was visibly, emotionally, physically, and spiritually rocked. But as for me and my trust in the Lord, after all, He's brought me through, how can I, the preacher and one he called, question anything? How could I ever question and feel the way I was feeling? I'm the one who heard an audible voice in 1983 and knew, without hesitation or reservation, God was using me for his kingdom. Yet, here I was, faith-rocked and questioning why God would do this to us. *Of all the cruddy things that have happened to our family, why give us something this devastating, so painful, and so downright cruel?*

None of us truly understands the depth of spiritual things that happen in life. We are tangible, physically oriented people. Spiritual things are less intrusive and less real to us. We talk about spirituality, and we want to be spiritual when it suits our needs, but in our fragile moments, we don't want to be spiritual. We want a reversal of the misfortune and to have the bad time we are going through fixed. Little did I know, God was taking the faith I had grown accustomed to and was reshaping it. He wanted me to grow deeper in him and increase my faith in him. He wasn't asking me for advice or wanting to have a conversation about it. God was forcing his hand to make it happen.

People of faith who strive to live by their creed of trusting God remove options from their thinking. Other people can come and go as they please in life. They can do things people deeply entrenched in their faith cannot do. To people of faith, doing what you want seems selfish and irresponsible because God has a different purpose in mind and a different call for them. Christ makes them grow deeper in their faith. Just ask the disciples who asked him to teach them how to pray and to increase their faith.

Martha's faith was shaken, and she needed the Lord. Her words to him, "Lord, *if* you had been here," were words of a woman whose faith was shaken. Her statement had two parts to it. Martha said, *"if."* This is a powerful word more associated with desperation than possibility. We have all had our *if* moments. Those times when our minds spun out of control, and our thoughts drowned in a fog. *If* this would have happened or *if* I would have done something differently. *If* I hadn't done that or *if* I would have done more. We play the if game without rationalizing that what was going to happen was going to happen. Martha's statement to Jesus spoke of both her faith having been shaken *and* her thirst for her to know what could have been different had he been there.

The other part of Martha's statement sounded like she was shifting blame. By saying *if* he had been there, she put the onus on him and removed the guilt from herself. Chances are, she felt an element of guilt. Her brother didn't die because of an accident or some misfortune. He died after having been sick. What *if* instead of placing the blame on Jesus, Martha would have acknowledged something else being done by her or Mary? Maybe they could have called in the physician sooner. Maybe they could have given him better medication or tended to his ailment with more urgency. Of course, this is all speculation, but it is a testament to the human psyche.

As we continued this journey with Jenn, Kathy and I learned a few things. One of the unfortunate pitfalls of stillbirths is the depth of guilt women feel. I say women because as Jenn's private pain became more public, many women came forward to share their stories. Women reached out through social media. Women would email her at work to share what had happened to them. Others shared their stories on her public Facebook page. There were cards and gifts sent with letters and testaments of what many of them had gone through.

And then there were the women of Hands of Faith Church. To our amazement, a good number of women shared their stories and their pain. Some gave details, but most simply shared a few words. Maybe they did this to guard against reliving the pain of the past while they were sharing. One woman spoke of the horror she experienced because of a doctor's lax attitude and dismissive approach. Had he been more attentive, maybe her baby would have been born alive and not asleep. Another woman shared about her loss and the response of the family around her. One woman said that after only a week, she was told to get over it and move on—her baby was dead, and there was nothing else she could do. One woman's family alienated her, and she felt alone. Many other stories were told, and all of them with one common theme—guilt ripped through them and tore them apart regularly.

Guilt is a word more felt than defined. Even within its definition is the word feeling. The *Cambridge Dictionary* defines it as "a feeling of having done something wrong." In every case, including Jenn's, each woman believed they did something wrong, causing hurt to their baby. In those moments, you can't tell someone not to *feel* guilty. Telling them not to feel is like telling someone not to breathe. If you feel guilty, it is because you feel guilty. Even if you did nothing wrong and even if nothing else could have been done, guilt still riddles you. It invades your thoughts and affects your heart and stress level by invading your emotions and causing you to feel its lingering effects at any moment and at any time. Warning signs don't show up and tell you that you are about to feel guilty. You feel guilty simply for living. Your reflection in the mirror is that of a guilty person. You talk to people, but your mind sees them talking to a guilty person. Though smiling at others, you believe they see through the façade and recognize your guilt.

In Martha's case, she couldn't live with the guilt. Instead of outlasting its sting, she decided to shift the blame. This trick is part of the human condition. It is an element of our sinful nature because it started in the Garden of Eden. When Adam and Eve ate the fruit and committed the sin of disobedience, God asked what they had done. Feeling guilty, Adam's first words were, "The woman you put here with me—she gave me some fruit from the tree, and I ate it" (Gen. 3:12). He shifted the blame because he knew he was guilty. Eve didn't make him eat, tell him he had to eat, or threaten him if he didn't. Adam knew the truth and knew God had made him responsible. Busted, you're guilty, and now you are shifting the blame. Adam wasn't the only one. God turned to Eve, the woman, and asked her what she had done. Her reply was, "The serpent deceived me, and I ate" (Gen. 3:13). Both shifted the blame from their sin to how they got the fruit. "Yeah, God, we ate it, but it was the woman; it was the snake. I didn't do it on purpose; I was made to do it. If you hadn't given me the woman, I wouldn't have done it. If you hadn't put that snake in the garden, I wouldn't have done it." Funny how the word *if* is still a part of the equation when we are shaken in our faith and how quickly we want to shift the pain and attention of our guilt onto someone else. Guilt, always unannounced, floods in and overwhelms the soul. At that point, your intention of shifting the blame changes. You are no longer in a vulnerable position but in a state of subtle anger, resentment, and even rebellion.

TEN

You Can't Keep a Good Man Down

The supreme happiness of life consists in the conviction that one is loved.

—Victor Hugo

Martha began her approach to Jesus, the Messiah, by calling him *Lord*. But in her weakened state of faith, her *if* moment resulted in her shifting guilt. She made a firm statement of conviction by emphatically stating, "My brother would not have died if you had been here." It was a statement, not a question, and it left no room for rebuttal by Jesus. There was no reasoning behind her words of conviction. Her words were personal, involved, and intimate. "My brother," not your friend, Mary's brother, the neighborhood's buddy, not the community's leader, but *my* brother. Martha was stating a fact: Lazarus was dead. What she implied is: Jesus, you weren't here. We can argue whose fault it is, but it still doesn't take away the fact Lazarus is dead. Jesus, you didn't meet my needs. I am not concerned right now with Mary or anyone else. Where were you when I needed you?

As we attended to Jenn's needs, it became clear to me after a few months that Gerald's needs had not been met. All our attention focused on Jenn, our daughter. But Gerald is our son-in-law and Miles' father. He lost a son. No, he didn't carry him or go through the pain of the C-section, but he was at that moment of stillbirth, holding his son, who was born sleeping. Gerald was there, unable to make the situation right and unable to fix what went wrong. He was present to hold his other children and tell them the horrible news. Every day, he picked up the pieces, cleaned the home, and felt lost in trying to know what to do about his wife. *How can I get her out of the abyss? How can I help her get through hell week? What can I do so she doesn't feel so guilty?* He likely felt like a failure.

I must say, though, I don't really know all Gerald was thinking; I am simply thankful for him being there. Some men may have left. Others may not have *been* tapped out but *would have* tapped out. He stayed. He stayed for Noah and Harper and to secure his home, marriage, and manhood. Gerald accepted the hand he was dealt. It would be wrong of me not to recognize his value in all this. He is a good man, raising a good family, with a good heart. This bad situation didn't turn him into a bad person. This I am grateful for.

I didn't directly ask Gerald, but through conversations, I know he had the *if* questions racing through his mind: *If I had done more for Jenn. If I had listened more to the doctor or paid more attention to the ultrasound. If I had made her eat more, sit more, walk less, hold Noah less, or carry Harper less.* The would-have, could-have statements and challenges made his grief more personal and painful. As personal as it was for Jenn, it was as personal for Gerald. And it was personal for Kathy and me. Kathy had her personal moments of losing her grandson. I had my personal moments of pain and fear, the pain of losing a grandson and the fear of praying to God to not lose my daughter.

I think the words "my brother" in the story of Jesus and Lazarus hit me a little harder because of my own brother. I felt Martha's angst and knew that tone of voice and the statement of conviction. If Jesus would have intervened, none of this, including my brother's death, would have happened. But Martha continued talking. Her words showed how she desired a different outcome. Martha wanted to make Jesus aware of her wishes and what should have been done.

Only Time Will Tell

In our finite minds and our temporary measure of lifespan, we constantly see the negativity of death and loss. Martha's words were not unreasonable. Not one of us, having lost a loved one, has not wished they wouldn't have died. I am sure Kathy, Philip, and Tony all wish their brother, Gregg, and their father, Dean, would not have died. I know my mother-in-law wishes her son and her husband would not have died. My sister-in-law, niece, and nephew wish that my brother, her husband, and their father would not have died. It's in us not to want to deal with death.

Martha continued both in her shaken faith and in her blaming Jesus. It is such a profound and assumptive statement she made: "If you had been here, my brother would not have died" (John 11:21). Are we sure if Jesus had been there, Lazarus wouldn't have died? How did she know this? Was she hoping, or was she in an angry stupor, speaking brash words? "If you had been here, my brother would not have died." What a sentence and what an indictment of how Martha was feeling and how she was projecting.

Shaken faith makes you do unconventional things. Blame makes you convey unconventional thinking. And assumptions make you process situations, resulting in unconventional actions. Martha was acting out, displaying her displeasure with the outcome of her brother with disdain for Jesus showing up. In her mind, had he been there, Lazarus would still be alive. I am not sure, but maybe Martha had even heard of how Jesus healed a little girl without even going to her home. Why? Why didn't he do the same thing for her brother?

Our emotions, at times, will get the best of us. We don't think clearly or properly. We say and think things that are out of character. But in the end, our raw emotions are telltale signs of who we are. Difficulties and tragedies will reveal the real person inside. As I read and studied Martha's words, I recognized myself in her image. I *thought* I was a man of faith, yet the faith I have was shaken. It let me know how much more growth I needed. I also realized, though I was not angry with God, I was angry about the situation God either allowed or put our family in. Like Martha, I needed more information, more answers, and a better understanding of what was happening.

As I wrote earlier, God can heal, bring back to life, and make situations right. He did it from cover to cover in the Bible. Were the stories I've read untruths? Is there such a thing as not having enough faith? Are the people who don't follow him right in their cynicism and critique that God is not just, that he is unfair? Is the person I am looking at in Martha really me in disguise? And just how do I get through these feelings? How do I not follow my emotions of anger and frustration? How do I not allow my mind to keep wandering and focusing on what I don't understand and what I lack in knowledge? I needed a revelation or some type of insight.

It seemed as if, no matter what I did, I was frozen in my pain and grief. I would pray, but no answer, at least no answer befitting my mood and mindset. I was no longer praying for the resurrection of Miles. I didn't realize until later that I had even stopped praying for Jenn—I was praying for myself. How could I help anyone else when I couldn't even help myself? What kind of preacher shares the gospel when he or she questions portions of what is written? Fortunately, I kept reading about Martha and continued to absorb her words. I listened to what she was saying to the Lord. I paid attention to her as if I were standing beside her at that moment.

Martha spoke five indelible words. These words became the impetus I needed. Martha's five words, in one phrase, helped me to see my faith was not shaken for the purpose of punishment. My faith was shaken to bring me closer to the Lord. "Come near to God, and he will come near to you" (James 4:8). Martha knew this before it was written. She went to meet Jesus—she was drawing near to him. And as she came near, he was drawing near to her. This is the necessary component for having your faith shaken. Draw near, and you will have what you need. And what I needed was a clear understanding of what our family was going through.

Strength and Courage Are Attainable

In three words, I can sum up everything
I've learned about life: it goes on.
—Robert Frost

The *Cambridge Dictionary* shares the word profound as an adjective, defined as "showing a clear and deep understanding of serious matters." I needed a profound statement to help me better understand what was happening within our family, give me insight into the grief we were experiencing, and tell me what God was doing within me. Why was I going through this emotional roller coaster? This is the kind of question you ask to begin your healing process. We need answers, but we also need to ask personal questions. It is a step towards a clear and deeper understanding of serious matters. It helps us when we find a profound statement.

I have not always been a sensitive person. I have been empathetic with people but never sympathetic. Maybe this was part of my learning curve—God developing me into a more sympathetic man so I could also be a better pastor. But did we, as a family, and did I, specifically, need this kind of pain to get to that point? Do any of us need that kind of pain? Do any of us need to learn about life's deepest grief to develop further as people? I had seen enough death and pain working in this area. And then I began to see the lesson. The more I looked and the more I kept reading Martha's words, I began to realize some new insights, which led me to my profound statement.

In some Christian circles, prophetic ministry is a regular part of the worship experience. Prophetic ministry is when God speaks to a person internally. Most often, a prophecy is conveyed about some future event taking place. It is a manner of foretelling a truth from God's perspective and from his Scripture coming to pass at some point in life. But there is another part of prophecy that isn't as glamorous or talked about quite as much. It is the forth-telling of the prophetic, known as the written word of God. Basically, it's the Bible. The Bible is a powerful benefit to us as believers because it can explain what is happening in the present from God's perspective. It strengthens us as his children to help us overcome whatever situation we may find ourselves in. It is not just a document relaying historical lives; the Bible is a living source of comfort when read and believed. The Bible, relaying Martha's words, was, in a way, God speaking to me. Through her words, God explained what I was feeling, how I was hurting, and what I was questioning.

As these words led me to God's purpose in my situation, I began to regain my strength. The Apostle Paul wrote, "We sent him to **strengthen** you, to **encourage** you in your faith, and to **keep you from being shaken** by the troubles you were going through." (1 Thes. 3:2-3, NLT, emphasis mine) Paul's young protégé, Timothy, was sent to help people who were in dire need. In his writing, Paul gave them and me this insight while also giving me a prophetic word in my time of need. Martha's words were there to strengthen me. To encourage me in my faith to go deeper. To help me not to be so shaken by future events in my life. This is not to say that I won't have other things in my life to shake me. What it says is that my *faith* won't be shaken. Each of us is shaken in some capacity whenever something out of the ordinary happens. We are blindsided and caught off guard, and we are shaken. But I learned despite such events, my faith grows deeper and is less inclined to be shaken, which strengthens me. Yes, my faith strengthens me. Not outside sources or words of friends. Not some substance for me to abuse, whether it be alcohol or drugs. Nothing can strengthen me in my time of need, like my faith and trust in knowing who God is. Martha's conversation changed my narrative. Her way of saying what was said is a powerful sentiment. Yet, there were more profound words to follow. Five more words caused my faith to shift and my focus to clear.

Let Us Begin Again

One kind word can change a person's day; a few kind words can change their life, and the right words, when spoken, can help change a person's situation.
—Unknown

When Martha first saw her friend, Jesus, she called him Lord. Next, she shared her anger and frustration and let it be known her faith had been shaken by saying, "*If* you had been here, my brother would not have died." Then, without warning or fanfare, she made a switch. She reclaimed her senses and rationality and continued her conversation with Jesus. She remembered whom she was speaking to and who could change everything within her situation, which included shifting her perspective on what was happening. *Martha had a restart.* With one three-letter word, she shifted. Martha's word after her revelation, after her restart, was the word *but.* And this was the first of the five words to my restart: but.

This word started the revelation and change in me. It is a simple word, and yet, it is a word used to contrast something already mentioned. In some places, it is a word of objection presenting an argument for something. Often, in Scripture, it is attributed to something God is about to do for his people. Preachers might share sermons on the "but God" Scriptures in the Bible. They are those moments when things seem hopeless and impossible, and then, without warning or alarm, God makes possible what was thought to be both impossible and improbable. It is a "but God" event. *"But God raised him from the dead"* (Acts 13:30, NLT). This referred to the resurrection of Christ. The author's previous words in this verse dealt with Christ being removed from the cross and placed in a tomb. But God raised him. God did the impossible and the improbable. He raised him from a lifeless body and made him alive again. It is a *but God* moment, the restart, the rejuvenation of lifelessness by which Martha tried to be encouraged. It is the same rejuvenation our family needed—I needed—to restart and regain focus, to re-energize my course of direction.

The word *but* is not only a contrast in speech. For Martha, me, and anyone, the word represents a change in direction. This change allows us to see what was previously hidden from us in our minds' eyes. Now we can hear words spoken before the word *but*. Words we couldn't hear because we were tone-deaf. Everything within our thought processes changes. We have a little more understanding of the whole picture because what we had done previously was to look at our situation in part. If all we do is look at the death and burial of Christ, then we can never rejoice in the resurrection. If all we speak of and pay attention to is his death and tomb experience, then we will miss the restart of the resurrection. His resurrection allowed for our access to God the Father. Because he came to life again, we have hope to live eternally and see our loved ones who lived for him and died in him.

Whenever we see the words *but God* in Scripture, we should take notice of a change about to happen. It was with this word *but* that Martha marked her change. It wasn't her looking for a change in the situation concerning Lazarus, or a change in Mary, or even a change in her life. It was her looking for a change in her pain and sorrow to turn into healing and joy.

What Do You Know?

You can't change your situation; the only thing you can change is how you choose to deal with it.
—Amanda Curiano

Stopping at the word *but* keeps us from seeing the full picture of how Martha transitioned. It keeps us from learning how our faith strengthens in times of weakness, sorrow, pain, and grief. Martha's subsequent words helped me find my place again in God's presence. Her words inspired me to sit and write the words on these pages. The words she spoke inspired my message for Easter Sunday morning, April 17, 2022. Martha followed her transitional word *but* with the words, *"Even now I know"* (John 11:22, NLT).

For me, in this season of sorrow, grief, hurt, and bewilderment, there were no more powerful words in God's Scripture than these; *even now, I know.* In the description of these words, I hear Martha saying, despite what has transpired and despite my most severe pain, my faith is growing stronger. Within me is the capacity to tap into faith so deep I can keep living and moving forward in life. I hear her, in her weeping and anger, saying, regardless of what may have transpired previously, there is something much deeper in me than I realized. I must dig down and live in that place. I heard the words quietly speaking, that I will not fully understand why Miles had to be born sleeping. The words told me how, in this season, our family would not be able to see the work being done right now. But we had to keep trusting in what God is doing because He knows the end of all things. We must keep living and moving forward because what we don't know, God knows.

It is difficult for all of us not to have answers to questions. We get frustrated with not knowing. Humans are, by nature, nosy. We must know things, understand them, and be aware of them. We don't like being left out of the loop. But when God is doing something, something much bigger and deeper than us, he tends not to let us in on the plan. I don't like it any more than the next person, but living by faith is about being able to trust God in the dark yet walking blindly in the direction of the Voice that calls you. Whether we like it or not, and whether we want to offer our opinion or not, is irrelevant to God. It's not that he doesn't care about us. He just doesn't care too much about how we think things should be done. Good parents always do what is best for their children. They will listen to the child whine, complain, and offer a variety of excuses to get what he or she wants. In the end, a good parent does what's best, even at the risk of the child being angry, hurt, upset, and dismissive.

When we are children, we don't understand the ways of our parents. We think they are mean and uncool, but we can't know the wisdom or experience they offer in trying to protect us. We have no idea they are doing things in our best interest. All we know is to throw tantrums and act out our displeasure, not being mature enough to handle their denials and demands. But then we grow up and begin to realize how much our parents really knew. We begin to realize what they know and see things from their vantage point. It's an epiphany to some small degree. We come to a place of knowing what we know, just like Martha came to herself. God knows, we know he knows, and that should be enough for us to keep moving forward and continuing to live.

Faith Is a Substance

No one knows what is going to happen in the next few minutes, and yet people still go forward because they have trust because they have faith.
—Paulo Coelho

Within each of us lives an element of faith. The non-biblical definition of faith simply means to have a belief in something with a strong conviction. It is having trust in something not necessarily tangible, and believing what you are trusting in will ultimately come to pass. For instance, we may say to a friend or co-worker, "I'll see you tomorrow." We trust, without reservation, that we will see that person. We don't think about or calculate the misfortunes that could take place before tomorrow. In these cases, we exhibit an element of faith. It is inherent in all of us. But faith doesn't keep us from experiencing bad things. It doesn't keep bad things from happening to us.

A friend of mine and I were driving to Columbus to play golf. We met up where he had parked his car and started our journey to the golf course. Ten miles from our destination, we found ourselves in a traffic jam. The problem wasn't the traffic jam; it was the two cars behind me rear-ending us that caused the problem. Never in our conversation did we consider our day being changed. I didn't start the trip thinking my car would incur more than five thousand dollars of damage. Fortunately, all parties were okay, and only the vehicles sustained damage. Our plans for the day changed. My responsibility for having to take care of my car changed from getting it washed to having it repaired. Faith told us we would go straight from Zanesville to Columbus to play golf. Life told us we would be on a detour and an unexpected situation would happen. None of us can ever predict life. But we can approach life through our faith.

As a Christian, I live knowing there is a different aspect to faith. Faith, in its simple form, makes itself active based on the object. In my auto accident, I had to activate my faith. In your unexpected life situation, you may have to activate your faith. When we put our faith in imperfect objects, we are inclined to be disappointed and let down. Christianity, however, has as our object none other than God himself. Activating my faith is being able to put my faith in God. Where we are sometimes unfaithful, God is always faithful. Scripture tells us his faithfulness is measurable (see Lam. 3:23, 1 Cor. 1:9, 10:13, 2 Thess. 3:3, and 1 John 1:9). These verses tell us one of God's absolute attributes is his being faithful, and Scripture also lets us see the sustainability of how faithful he is because it never fades away but remains always (2 Tim. 2:13). When God is the object of our faith, there is an understanding even when our faith is shaken, God remains the same—*faithful*. When we aren't sure of whom we can trust or what we believe, God raises our awareness of his presence so we can know he is there. He wants us to know we are not alone.

Where's Your Focus?

*God hears, and He sees, and you are not alone in your
struggles. Remain firm and stable, for God has
your deliverance planned.*
—Joyce Meyer

Martha felt alone when her brother died. This was the
case when Jesus wasn't there when Miles died. And it may
be the case when you lose someone you love. Perhaps the
situation is trying to derail you and shake your faith. At
least, it may seem that way. In Martha's case, she didn't see
Jesus or know where he was. When we don't feel or see him,
we think he is not there in our loss either.

We think in terms of time and space. We impose limits and
boundaries on God and believe he only shows up at certain
moments. Well, our situations are not an indicator of God's
inability to be everywhere. Just because we don't feel him or
see him doesn't mean he isn't present. Bad things happening
to us don't contradict his faithfulness. Jesus knew what the
outcome for Lazarus would be. He also knew the reaction
and responses he would receive when he showed up. For
Martha, Jesus was late, and that lateness shook her faith, and
she became angry. She felt betrayed, isolated, insignificant,
disrespected, and irrelevant. I don't say this as someone who
was with Martha at that moment, but rather as one who felt
the same way when I didn't know if God was in our loss and
pain. I said it as one who felt betrayed, let down, insignificant,
irrelevant, and ignored as I pled with God and begged him
for his presence and miracle-working hand to be present.
Not at some later date, but now, at that moment, for him to
be present. All I was experiencing was emptiness, a loss of
feeling, and a loss of awareness of what was going on.

There may be times in your life you may wonder where God is. You may not sense his presence. It seems he is distant and nonexistent in your pain and grief. I am not an expert on the human psyche, and maybe I should have done more research, but during those moments of pain and grief, we turn more to how we feel than to what we know. Our feelings are a part of our flesh, the part of us making us aware of ourselves. When we hurt, cry, feel discouraged, or are in despair, we are entrenched in ourselves more than anyone or anything else. Our focus is on our pain and what caused the pain. We are not in a position to be aware of other human beings, let alone be aware of God. But rest assured, if you are a child of God, he is there.

On occasion, my girls would fall and hurt themselves. They would come screaming into the house, looking for their mother or me. Their focus, however, would be on what caused their pain. We would clean the scrape, hold them, cuddle with them, and yet, they would still talk about the wound.

When Jenn was lying in her bed, unable to get out of the dark bedroom and reengage in life, her mother and I would hold her. We would go in and pray with her. Her children, Noah and Harper, would go in and check on her. Gerald would try his best to tend to her. But her focus was on her pain. She was deeply hurting in a way only other women in her place could understand. Her focus was not on God, her family, her health, or even her body. Her focus was on her baby boy, whom she would never hold again on this side of Heaven. She focused on her loss, pain, grief, and sorrow. And in those few moments of conversation, she would ask her pastor-dad, where is God? Where is he, and why doesn't he answer me? If he had been here, maybe my boy would not have died.

ELEVEN

When You See Him, You See

*The worst feeling in the world is knowing you did the best
you could, and it still wasn't good enough.*

—Unknown

King David understood heartache and brokenness. "Is anyone crying for help? God is listening, ready to rescue you. If your heart is broken, you'll find God right there; if you're kicked in the gut, He'll help you catch your breath" (Psalm 34:17-18, MSG). We don't always feel like those words are real or soothing, but they are factual. God is in our broken hearts. He hears our cries, sees our tears, and listens to our sobbing and weeping. God is ready to breathe life back into our empty lungs, lungs that are depleted from losing our breath in our grief. If we can find a way to shift our focus from our flesh, then we can accept the caress of his presence in us. We can know he is there.

God is not in the habit of hiding from his children. Jesus wasn't hiding from Martha; he wasn't even delayed. He simply showed up at a different time than she desired. But he came to her in her brokenness and grief. Jesus came after Lazarus died, not when he was sick. Jesus could have healed Miles in Jenn's womb when the placenta was attached to the uterus, but he didn't. He came when our hearts were broken to soothe and ease our pain, and he will do the same for others. When Martha heard Jesus was coming, she went and met him (John 11:20). Though he was on his way to allow her to experience his presence, she had to meet him where *he* was and not where *she* was.

Getting out of our own way is hard to do. It is harder to do when we are in pain and more difficult still when we are in deep grief. But then, we see a small glimmer of hope, the moment of clarity when we see Jesus. Not tangibly, of course, and not even in our spiritual state of existence. No, we see him in our brokenness and our pain. Isn't that what King David said? If our heart is broken, we'll find God right there. When we exhaust all other options, we have an opportunity to find him. Once our reservoir of tears has been drained, we begin to see him through renewed sight. When we call out to or run out of questions for him, we can listen to the tenderness of the Holy Spirit whisper to us, "He, your heavenly Father, is right here." It's when we need him most that God comes, in full force, to occupy all of us.

The Apostle Paul's benediction to the church at Corinth in his second letter gives us insight. He wrote, *"The grace of the Lord Jesus Christ, and the love of God, and the communion of the Holy Spirit be with you all"* (2 Corinthians 13:14, NKJV). There is grace, a favor, a blessing that comes from the Lord Jesus Christ and rests upon us. The warming embrace of the Father's love surrounds us and brings us a comforting peace no human hug can duplicate. We are able to fellowship and be in harmony and union with the Holy Spirit, who is known as the Comforter. He spends quality time with us, quietly and gently removing the sting of our pain so that we can know the love of the Father and the favor of the Son. For the children of God, there is never a time he is not near—we are never alone. We may *feel* alone or think he is *far away*, but in the broken heart of pain, we will find him, all of him—the Father, the Son, and the Holy Spirit.

When Jesus showed up for Martha, the conversation most likely went as he suspected it would. It was the same conversation I had with him, "Jesus, if you had been here, Miles would not have died." But as it was with Martha, I had a similar element of surprising revelation, where my faith kicked in and made me recognize Martha's inherent trust and belief in Christ—the kind of faith which allowed me to utter the same words Martha used. They were the words that led to my revelation and began the healing process for my soul: *"Even now, I know."*

Knowledge Is a Gift—Don't Waste It

> *Faith is a knowledge within the heart,*
> *beyond the reach of proof.*
> —Khalil Gibran

What is it I began to know? What was it I would come to know? What was the revelation leading to my restart? What led me to my refreshment of spirit?

There is a difference between what is *instinctive* (impulsive, spontaneous, without thinking) and what is *inherent* (a natural part of our humanity). The news of Miles' death initiated an emotional outburst. It didn't happen initially, but when it did, it came from inside of me. There was never a thought-out manifestation of tears. I simply started weeping profusely and couldn't stop until I stopped. My tears happened by instinct. They were instantaneous. But after the emotion had passed, my instinct turned into an inherent need to know. My humanness took over, and I desired to tap into a depth of understanding going beyond my level of intellect. What transpired was a spiritual experience of seeing Martha's words become my words, and my words make sense out of what seemed senseless.

Yet, what was it I was beginning to know? What was God showing me, and what did I have in common with Martha? And though I desired to know the whys of what happened to Miles, life doesn't often answer the unanswerable questions. The doctors and science don't have all the answers. To this day, we don't know what happened in Miles' situation. But what I do know is Christ showed me himself and what was necessary to understand the eternal elements of life. He showed me what was written in the fine print of his word and what it means to be a person of faith. To all my questions, God showed me three aspects to help me understand what was happening. I was beginning to learn that these three aspects can help each of us begin our healing process and capture the essence of what we already know.

He Was Already There

First, when Jesus showed up and was approached by Martha, Martha made him aware of the situation. However, before being present, Jesus was *already* aware of the situation. When

Jesus had heard of Lazarus being sick, he stated, "This sickness is not unto death, but for the glory of God . . ." (John 11:4, NKJV). Jesus knew Lazarus was going to die. But he also knew Lazarus wasn't going to stay dead. We are the ones unaware of the entirety of the picture. We don't know the whole story. On the other hand, Jesus was fully aware of everything happening.

With our limitations and restrictions of time and space, sometimes we ignore the timelessness of God. God exists in infinity, but we think in finite terms. We speak of how long something lasts, yet God speaks of all that is everlasting. Like Martha, we think he shows up when we see him. We forget he was there before we even thought of him.

As a pastor, *I know* God is omnipresent everywhere at the same time. We may not understand it, nor are we even able to comprehend it, let alone live as if we are aware of it. But God is transcendent, going beyond time, space, and matter. Romans 1:20 tells us though God is invisible, he has shown us his qualities through what is seen on earth and in the sky. He is made known to us because all of nature has manifested his essence. He is the Creator of all, and nature expresses his hand of existence. As a pastor, *I know* God is always with me, even if I don't feel him or see him, because faith has taught me this truth. The reality is, as a man of faith, my relationship with the Lord is not predicated upon my subjection of whether he is or isn't, or whatever it is he does or doesn't do. The entirety of my relationship is based upon the fact that God is, and God does as he pleases through his sovereignty.

This is what *I know*, inherently and instinctively. Although it may not be your truth, or maybe you haven't come to this truth just yet, it is the truth. Both from faith and experience, *I know* the fact God is always present.

Unlike Martha, I don't need to see him walking towards me or hear he is in town for me to come running. I don't have to look in the mirror (though I do) or read my Bible to know he is with me. All I do is look within my heart, whether it is broken or whole, and know he has taken up residence. I don't know about Martha, but I do know I am saved by grace. One of my favorite Bible verses tells us Christ lives in us (Gal. 2:20). And Paul repeats the same thing in another chapter (2 Cor. 13:5). Christ lives in us. It is my truth. And it is truer to me now than ever before.

There are other things I should know, things that are certain to me and my faith. I should know God would never leave me hanging. I should know I am not alone, and my pain and agony are not foreign to him. Hebrews tells us he sympathizes with our weaknesses (Heb. 4:15). On the cross, he identified with moments of our feeling abandoned when he cried out to the Father about being forsaken. I should know all these things. The problem is pain, grief, sorrow, sadness, heartache, and brokenness alter your thought processes. They take you out of your spiritual zone and remind you of your humanity and natural condition of rebellion toward God. If not for the Spirit of God and the salvation of God, I would stay in that condition of despair. But because of what I know, according to his promise, he will never leave me or abandon me (Deut. 31:6 and John 14:18).

These are facts I know but must be reminded of. Martha's words—*even now I know*—reminded me that in my weakest, most vulnerable, heartbroken condition, I know God is with me. It is not my hope nor my wish; it is his stated promise and my deep conviction. He is with me till the end. He is also with you—in your pain and grief, your heartache and sorrow, and your most trying moments of despair. Hopefully, you will come to know this. For me, this is what I should have known. This is what *even now I know*.

Look for Him

Second was the recognition and revelation of who Jesus is beyond what he can do. Martha made a true statement of belief about what she knew. "Lord, if you had been here, my brother wouldn't have died." (John 11:21, NIV) It is the same statement I whispered to myself in the hospital room, "Lord, if you are God, Miles didn't die; he is just sleeping, so wake him up. You can do this. You can do all things. I know you can." Jesus didn't raise Lazarus, and he didn't raise Miles.

When Martha saw him, she wanted him to do something. Not later, when it was convenient or when things calmed down, but at that moment. We all long to avoid pain, sorrow, and grief. We want Jesus to do what he did in the Bible—perform miracles. He was always messing with people's minds when he ministered. He would turn water into wine and not drink it. He cast out demons by speaking and healed a blood-diseased woman without touching her. He healed a child from a distance, fed thousands with little food, walked on water, and overwhelmed Peter's nets with fish.

Knowing his miracle-working power, Martha made a reasonable statement. I can envision her saying, "Jesus, if you had been here, you could have performed a miracle on my brother, and he wouldn't have died. If you had just *done* your thing, I wouldn't be crying my eyes out and hurting like I am." Oh, Martha, how well I understand your frustration.

We are like children who want toys from Santa. We promise to be good to get the toys, not because we want to know Santa. From God, we want blessings, benefits, the good stuff, and none of the bad. We want God to *do it* for us when we ask and done in a way that suits us. We ask him for stuff and commit to going to church, tithing, singing louder, being nicer, and making other promises we know we won't keep. Don't get me wrong; God blesses his children. He blesses us more than our earthly fathers (Luke 11:13). But he wants to bless us because we come to him for him, not for what he brings with him.

What I should have known, and what I do know, is God wants me to want him, and in wanting him, he blesses me with the stuff. It says it right there in Hebrews, "For he who comes to God must believe that he is, and he is a rewarder of those who diligently seek hi*m*" (Heb. 11:6, NKJV). God responds and blesses those who seek him and not his stuff.

Martha did one thing right. She went out and met him. She sought him out. The interaction and answers Martha was looking for came because she went looking for Jesus. She knew it was him she needed, even if her continued sentiment questioned his timing. Though she still wanted her stuff—her brother to be alive—she knew, first and foremost, she needed Jesus. What Martha recognized is what I had a revelation of—I needed Jesus. Holding Miles in my arms, kissing his cold cheeks, breathing my breath into his nostrils, clutching and drawing him closer to my chest, and crying out to God were all worthy, relevant, and biblical practices and beliefs. But they weren't Jesus. When nothing happened, and no miracle was performed, I needed Jesus. What I wanted was misguided. Does Jesus heal? Yes. Could he have healed Miles? Yes. Was it within his purpose and plan? Apparently not.

In those moments of revelation, when God *isn't* going to do something, we must refocus ourselves away from what we wanted God to do and look at who he is. Sometimes we are so caught up in the miracles of the Bible we overlook the real parts of people's lives. Jesus didn't heal everyone or feed everyone. And here's an epiphany: He didn't save everyone. People still died in Jesus's time. Children died; parents and whole families died. People went hungry, and families were at odds. Politics were crooked, and discrimination against women and people of color existed even then.

The truth is Jesus didn't walk around and interact with people for what he could do. When he performed a miracle, he would tell the people not to say anything (Mark 1:41-44). He told people not to go around spreading stories about their healing or deliverance. People came to him for free food (John 6:26-27), and he turned the conversation into a sermon about Heaven and eternal life. He challenged them to want what he could give them with his life instead of them wanting what he could give to them in this life. Jesus will always say, "Want me," before he will let us know what he can do for us. This was my revelation. It was what Martha recognized and what *even now I know*.

This, Too, Shall Pass

Third, there is a reality of time and space operating at different levels when we compare temporal versus eternal. In Martha's case, she was adamant about Jesus not being there. His seemingly lax attitude and tardiness created her grief and sorrow at the loss of her brother. Not wanting to read into her emotions and feelings, I'll simply say that in Jenn's hospital room and the days that ensued, my annoyance at God's timing or lack thereof was extremely emotionally charged. Anger, frustration, hurt, irritability, as well as being distraught and discouraged were some of the emotions I felt during that time. When facing a trauma, you act out and react according to the situation causing it. Yes, you cry and yell, and you feel agony and gut-wrenching pain. You don't make plans or have conversations about anything futuristic because the present is too intense with feelings of sorrow and despair. Words like "this, too, shall pass" mean nothing to you. You don't hear anything, you cannot see straight, you are unable to speak, and you just hurt. And your hurt is unrelenting. It is measurable, real, and there in the moment. For me, it seemed as if it would never go away.

Our bodies ache with pain. Pain invades every part of our being. Unfortunately, our bodies will not last forever. The Bible is clear. Our outward man, our flesh, is dying every day, but the inward man, our spirituality, is being renewed and made stronger. It is being prepared for eternity for those who are born again (2 Cor. 4:16). We live in the temporary, the now moments of life (2 Corinthians 4:18). We live to seize the day or, at least, make plans for a few weeks or months ahead. But God doesn't deal with the temporary. He is in our temporary situations, but he doesn't dwell there. God lives in the eternal, the ever-existing place of time never-ceasing. He doesn't make decisions. He doesn't operate with a plan to satisfy us. His work for and through us is always considering eternity. But in grief and sorrow, we don't think about eternity; we only think about the now.

Martha thought about the now. Our family thought only about the now. In her words, Martha alluded to the now when she said, "Even now." But God exists in the everlasting from everlasting, from the eternal to the eternal. The Apostle Paul said, "For our light affliction, which is but for a moment, is working for us a far more exceeding and eternal weight of glory" (2 Cor. 4:17, NKJV). God wants our attention to be eternal, even in a temporary situation. This is difficult for our minds to comprehend. Our lives should look heavenward during our most painful times of life, not in the temporal troubles of life. But that's exactly what needs to be done to pull us through. When we see Jesus and look to eternity, we are reminded he *is* the resurrection and the life. He doesn't do resurrections—he *is* the resurrection. It is in him we have fundamental lessons of knowing we'll see our loved ones again who have died in him. Knowing this may not ease the physical and emotional pain of the moment, but it is what begins the healing process from our spirit as our bodies and minds catch up.

A Vision Unlike Any Other

Last, the final element of what even now I know is the intrinsic, deep-seated, spiritual presence of the Holy Spirit in me. This awareness became real during this most traumatic and painful time in my life. It was mid-November, barely a month removed from Miles. The pain was still fresh and real. It was then the most spiritual and surreal moment occurred.

Kathy has always been a fan of Michael Bublé. (I think it's because he has the same initials as me and has nothing to do with his ability to sing.) But being the loving husband that I am, I purchased tickets to his concert in Cincinnati and gave her the good news on Mother's Day 2020. Because of the pandemic, it would be a whole year and a half before we could cash in on the tickets. The date of the concert was set months in advance. And for all those months, she looked forward to it. But now, with Miles' stillbirth, I wasn't sure of what to do. However, she wanted to go, thinking it would be a small distraction for the two of us to refresh and gather ourselves for a few moments.

The night of the concert was rainy. November's chill was in the air, and we felt every bit of it as we stood in the long line leading us into the arena. Workers were checking for masks and all the COVID credentials, so it took a little longer than normal. While the trip to Cincinnati was relatively uneventful, the conversation was light. We stood in line and mostly listened to the surrounding people, so we stood in silence. We were still numb and unsure of whether it was okay to be happy and enjoy our time out. I also knew most of Kathy's thoughts remained on Jenn, Gerald, Noah, Harper, and, of course, Miles. Finally, we made our way into the arena and found our seats. As the orchestra played and Michael sang, our minds were finally able to be removed from the last several weeks. I saw joy on Kathy's face for the first time in a while. It lifted my spirits, and I realized I, too, had relaxed. Though I enjoyed the singing, I had more fun watching the musicians in the orchestra and their skillfulness. As with most concerts, intermission came, and we stood to stretch our legs. I remember Kathy hugging me and thanking me. We, unfortunately, reconnected to the pain of our season and how hard it was to let go of the grief to gain a glimpse of joy again. As the lights came up, Kathy was finally able to see my face. She realized I had been crying and asked me if I was okay.

It was only moments before the intermission that my spiritual event took place. Michael started singing the song "Home," made famous by him and Blake Shelton. Along with the song, he showed a video. But it wasn't just the song or the video; it was the vision God showed me that hit me hard. I will never forget, for as long as my mind stays right, the vision God gave me, producing both joy and sorrow. Both emotions flowed through me at the same time. It was a moment of spiritual awareness of God's presence in a way I've never experienced in all my years of being a Christian.

Also in my spiritual moment, I realized that grieving and living with loss will never go away. Grief has a variety of mannerisms and methods by which it produces itself. But it never really leaves you. You simply learn how to live with whatever expression it prefers to show itself. You learn to handle each day as it happens.

There we were, Kathy and I, both laughing and hugging at the same time. We were hurting, and we were fighting for solace, and yet we found a moment of joy. Later, I felt guilty for separating myself from the grief for a few moments. No one tells you about feeling guilty. Our culture and society have told us, through movies and dramatic events, how we should feel and what we should feel. We've been shaped and molded into categories, so if we laugh during our grief, we feel guilty because it is too soon to laugh. On the flip side, we've been instructed not to go too long without laughing or having fun because then it becomes detrimental to our mental health.

We do these things because we live in the temporary, restrictive moments of life. But because God is not limited by time, he shows up at the most unexpected times and takes you to places you may have never been before. What did he show me, causing my joy and sorrow to collide? What was the vision just before the intermission, during the song "Home," that broke me from living in my pain of the flesh to finding joy in my spirit?

As with most large concerts, the lights in the arena are off for the audience. The only lights are those on the stage and, in this case, those on the screens around the arena. As Michael sang "Home," images of loved ones hugging and embracing each other scrolled through. The actors on the screens showed the joy of seeing each other. But then, out of nowhere, God seemingly placed before me a separate screen. The screen then split in two, and behind the screen was a curtain that parted. As the curtain parted, it revealed a young man. He was light-skinned and muscular, not to the point of bodybuilder strength but toned and well-built. He was about six feet one inch to six feet two inches tall, with a solid jawline, and extremely handsome. As I saw him, very deep within me, deeper than any other place I had ever felt within my body, I knew it was Miles. Yet, as sure as I was, I wasn't sure. But then, above the orchestra and Michael's crooning voice, he spoke to me. In a simple sentence, he said, "Nonno, I'm fine. Let them know I am fine. Let them all know I am fine."

Of course, at that moment, I wasn't fine. The floodgates of tears began to gush again. I had discovered a spiritual place I had never known before. That was when I knew the God of the resurrection was about eternity and not the temporary. It was when I knew God was in each moment of our pain and cared enough about our hurt that he allowed for an exchange between Miles and me. And then, without warning or fanfare, Miles was gone again. The curtain closed, the screen vanished, and I was back in the arena listening to Michael finish his song. But then, another spiritual moment happened. I heard two non-clinical words whispered in my ears. When I heard it in my heart and mind, I held on to it and typed it in my notes on my cell phone. I wanted to look it up and know what it meant clinically or from a counseling perspective.

Days later, when I decided to research the words I heard, I couldn't find them. Separate words joined together in harmony as one. I found them individually. I found the definition for each. But I did not find them linked together.

Only in my hearing and in my heart were they together and real. The words *euphoric grief* came to me. In that instance, when I saw Miles, both the euphoria of seeing him and the pain of seeing him overwhelmed me at the same time. It was a moment in which I was jealous because of the splendor and perfection of the surrounding images. I glimpsed glory and how perfect Miles was. I saw a life having never known pain or the difficulties of living in this world. In him, I saw what I longed for: peace, calm, unconditional love, warmth, kindness, and tenderness. All I wanted to do was hug him, yet in my jealousy, I hurt because I wanted the moment to last. I couldn't have what he had. I also grieved because I couldn't get to him and ask him questions. All I could do was stand there and soak it all in.

Time was standing still. The clock may have been ticking on my watch, but in eternity, time stands still. I was caught up in a place of stillness while activity and motions happened around me. Michael and his song continued, but time and motion had slowed to almost a complete stop. It was euphoria, and yet it was grief. It was a euphoria embraced by grief—*euphoric grief*. I had never experienced a feeling like it before, nor have I experienced it since. This is another unexplainable element of being a person of faith, trying to make sense of the unexpected and unexplainable. We realize that God goes beyond all our mental faculties and invades our space, time, and matter. We know now, even now, God has his hand in everything, even the most painful of things, to increase the fortitude of our faith in him.

Expect the Unexpected

A few months after the concert, I had an unexpected conversation. I had been thinking about euphoric grief and how silly a phrase it seemed when I received a text from my friend Kim asking if she could share something with me that seemed odd and yet very real to her. Her mother had just passed away unexpectedly. Kim was, of course, in grief and had to handle the arrangements for her mom's funeral. She was also tasked with finding the right burial spot for her mom's final resting place. As she walked through the cemetery, her thoughts were on her dad, brothers, and how she would get through the next few days. Then she found a spot she thought her mom would best be honored, but she was unsure. In an instant, a butterfly flew up next to her. Spotting it, she began to feel a warmth, and peace came over her. She was feeling both joy and sadness at the same time. She wanted to laugh and cry in the same breath.

In her inquiry to me, she wanted to know if what she felt made any sense or if she was being emotionally crazy. She was feeling euphoria and grief at the same time. She was crying in sorrow and joy together as one emotion. Little did Kim know in sharing her experience with me, she helped calm my insecurity about what I had experienced. She confirmed to me what I believe God gives us in those moments of weakness and frailty—*euphoric grief*. I don't know if others have ever experienced such a thing or if others ever will, but I do know it is real to me, and it is real to Kim. Because of it, I am thankful to God for his amazing grace to us all.

What's Next?

Reading the entirety of the verse, Martha said more than "even now I know." She had a continuation of her initial phrase. She said further, "But even now I know that whatever You ask of God, God will give You" (John 11:22, NKJV).

In other words, Martha's sentiment was that no matter what has transpired previously, and no matter what did or didn't happen, her faith is not in what may happen. She may have said, "My faith, Lord, is in you. Whatever you decide, Jesus, whatever you determine, whatever happens next, it's because you are God." Obviously, I wasn't there to know how the exchange went nor how Martha sounded or looked. But putting myself in her shoes, I knew how she felt.

The range of emotions is intense and varied as we navigate our grief, and it feels surreal as we try to move from sadness to laughter again. This time can even be unnerving because it seems as if we may have forgotten how to laugh. It feels uneasy and foreign in some ways. Guilt tries to work its way back in. And we tire from the battle of working our way back to joy. The entirety of our journey was met with tears and laughter. Our family had times of silent weeping and verbal reassurances, along with private and public conversations. The whole of this crisis created a mixture of highs and lows and every feeling in between. But like Martha, I realized I had no control over any other tragedy in my life or our family's lives. I simply knew, for whatever reason, Miles was not with us.

To this day, I have no idea why he was taken from us. But as Martha said, "Lord, you are God." For some people, that's not a reassurance. But for those who understand the depth of God's workings, we know God has answers to questions we don't know exist. God also has thoughts and ways we will not understand. We continue in our relationship with him, knowing he is God and we are not. Even now, I know God's answer to my question is simply, "I am God. Trust me."

TWELVE

An Ongoing Transition

There is no greater agony than bearing
an untold story inside of you.

—Maya Angelou

There is more to the story of Martha and Jesus and the message it conveys. But this is not the time for it. This is a story about our family. It is also a reflection of the stories of all the women who have ever lost a child through stillbirth. This is a heart-wrenching story about pain, grief, sorrow, and sadness. It is the story of Jenn, Gerald, Noah, and Harper, but also about Pamela, Kendall, K'Niyah, Michael, and Jakobi. It is our story, too, Kathy's and mine. And the story is still unfolding as we transition from grief to being thankful for having each other. It is our story of spending quality time together, laughing lightly, crying deeply, and then learning to laugh intensely. It is a beautiful thing to see Jenn laughing again, seeing her and her sister sharing memes and Instagram® photos, laughing from deep down inside. But then solitary moments of soft tears remind us we are still on a journey of healing. We tell each other's story of how we are transitioning from grief to realizing how grateful we are for our family. It is a powerful story we wanted to tell in hopes others can find their family as well.

As our story goes on, it is also our story of Miles. It is about how we have connected with many other stories of women and families who have lost babies through stillbirths. I have taken it upon myself to write about it. I'm sure there are other books dealing with stillbirth and infant mortality. But this is our story from our vantage point of faith and our position of pain. In truth, I didn't research the subject of stillbirths to see if anyone else has ever written about their experience. I didn't want to, not because I don't respect anyone else's pain, but because I didn't want to be influenced by what someone else may have said. I wanted to present the topic from my perspective, Jenn and Pamela's perspective, and from our family's perspective collectively. Still, there are other perspectives within the story. I wanted to share how our faith was tested and how our family had to push through. I wanted you, the reader, to know how we went extremely low in our emotions and are still climbing out. It was within my heart to let you know how we faced an unexpected tragedy and couldn't stop life. We couldn't stop ministering. We couldn't stop breathing. It is our story, but with hope and prayer, it will shed light on the challenges of others who have stories to tell.

It is our story prayerfully to enlighten those in the health profession to see the mental, emotional, and physical strain of what families go through in a different kind of loss. Unlike the loss of an aging parent or an adult child, the loss of a silent birth child is different. I've lost a parent and a brother, and other family members, and I am truly thankful I have not lost a child. But I did lose a grandchild. And as any grandparent can tell you, grandchildren are different. As a pastor, I have done more than my fair share of funerals. I have stood with families on every occasion, sometimes weeping with them, other times, withholding my tears to allow them to finish with theirs. I can honestly tell you I have never experienced pain like the morning Jenn called to tell us Miles was gone, and I have never begged, pleaded, and threatened God in the manner I did when I held our precious baby boy. I have never wanted God to intervene and be the resurrector he said he is more than at that moment of loss. Miles' death took a toll on us mentally and physically, unlike anything else in this life.

The health profession needs to know what families go through physically, financially, emotionally, and, in our case, spiritually. It was hard for Jenn to stay in the hospital maternity ward. She had lost her baby and had to listen to other families giddy over theirs. She had to keep listening to new mothers and fathers speak of the color of their baby's eyes and endured the conversations of new grandparents, excited and making their excitement known. To have to keep listening to the life of other children around you is another level of pain. I keep hoping hospital administrators hear our plea to make a change—to hear the cries of the mothers who have lost a child and the families who are grieving. Maybe we can all be more in tune with one another's grief and one another's pain.

Maybe some agencies need to be more aware of the trauma and desperation families go through to understand and regain their sense of well-being to live again. Maybe health agencies or hospitals can collaborate a little more to help grieving families recover and find some normalcy in living again. Or maybe there can be more funding or research to discover the reasons for infant mortality so that we can decrease the number of families experiencing such sorrow and pain. But that is for another book or another person to answer these statements.

But even now, I know, despite not having answers nor fully understanding the reasons, I at least have a deeper conviction of God's grace. I have come to realize the privilege of being in a relationship with the Most High God. I can, without reservation, attest to my family's tenacity and courage through our trust in Christ. Without hesitation, I can attest to the comforting presence of the Holy Spirit on the days I couldn't feel my face or connect to any other human being.

The Mind Is Both Fragile and Agile

Miles' story will go on. Other stories about stillbirth and other families out there need health professionals to reach them. This is also a story about recovery and regaining a sense of purpose in life. It is about being able to feel again, allowing yourself to laugh, smile, and be happy. It is about finding joy in the Lord and joy in the life he has given you.

There is a mental toll the families go through as well. Jenn is one of the strongest women I have had the privilege of knowing, her mother being the first and her sister being the second. These are amazing women of God. Resilient, resourceful, and resolute in every aspect of life. They are all successful women, and I am proud to be in the mix of their existence. But as strong as they are and as much fortitude as they possess, this broke them. As women and mothers, they were broken mentally, emotionally, and spiritually. But I am thankful they did not stay broken. Their support systems of work families, church families, friends, colleagues, relatives, and some strangers have helped them. It has helped all of us to keep climbing higher and to be better because of it.

But there is also another element to this equation, not to be dismissed or overlooked. Gerald, Kendall, and I, as men, have struggled mentally and are a part of this story too. I cannot put us in the same category as our women because we can never feel or experience what any woman goes through in giving birth. But as men, when we can't fix something or solve something, we suffer mental anguish. We feel like failures and a little less manly. We label ourselves as unable to provide for the safety and security of our families. As men, we are labeled unemotional because we don't cry enough, don't show enough sympathy, and don't seem broken even though we are. Although we may not be able to show it, we become mentally fatigued and unable to function.

And so, this story, our story to the mental health industry, counselors, and clinicians, is to let them know people are suffering. Men, women, children, and whole families of survivors of silent births, have made the journey to health successfully. But for every family that has made it, whether because of their support system or because of time, many more families haven't made it. Families are still suffering, still climbing out, still trying to find answers to their questions, and still trying to gain an understanding of the unreasonable. Families struggle to find a resolution, and though we don't have the numbers, stillbirths affect countless lives every year.

My hope is for something more to be done to help women, men, and families who go through such pain. As I shared our story with friends and even strangers, they began to tell me of someone they knew and how hard or sad it was watching them go through such a trauma. Our family is truly grateful for the care and compassion Jenn and Gerald received during her days in the maternity ward at OSU. But when she was being discharged, they gave her papers and pamphlets to let her know that if she needed to talk to someone, there were a few agencies available. Unfortunately, it wasn't the hospital's responsibility to follow up.

Fortunately, Jenn has a support system. And she continues to heal every day. But what about those women and families without a support system? Who follows up with them? Where do they go to find healing or funding to get financial support for time off work? Who helps them pay their hospital bills? Who is there for the single mom or the couple whose families are in another location? The more I heard, the more my heart hurt for those not getting the emotional and mental help they needed. If we have agencies and facilities for those caught in addiction, those who attempt suicide, or others who grieve for a family member they've lost, then how do we get these agencies to realize a stillbirth is different? Sufferers of stillbirths need help too. I can't explain it all, and I hope this book helps to bring a little light to the emotional, mental, physical, and spiritual toll it takes on even a strong family like ours. I wrote this book in hopes of helping to make strides and to make a difference in the lives of those families still clinging to life from their unfortunate loss. My prayer is this can happen sooner rather than later.

To those families who have not made it out or are still climbing, I don't have a medical answer for your loss. I don't have any psychological insights or clinical formulas to step you through. But here is what I have to offer you. In the

Gospel of John, Martha responds to Jesus's words about him being the resurrection. He asks her if she believes. She responds with three imperatives that have become my mantra through this journey of ours. These words are what helped me know how to continue healing and helping. Martha said, "Yes, Lord, I believe that You are the Christ, the Son of God, who is to come into the world" (John 11:27, NKJV). The three imperatives are:

1. Believe in Christ.
2. Know he is the Son of God.
3. Know he came to save lives by giving up his.

In these fundamental statements, I try to live my life. It is what gets me through difficult days and the frustrations that come with life. It is the extension of Martha's words, "Even now I know," speaking to my belief in Christ as my Lord. He knows what I am going through, and he cares about me personally, not just in a collective manner with the rest of mankind. He knows me, he loves me, and he created me for his purpose. When I believe this truth, and when I believe in him, I find comfort in knowing he knows the course of my life. He is the Son of God that expresses both his deity and his uniqueness. There is no other son. There are no other actual children, only those of us who have been adopted. And because of our adoption, we are a part of the family of God, connected eternally to the Son of God, who set the tone for our being able to endure this world's problems and pains.

The first two statements are based upon the third: *He gave up his life for us to have life eternally*. Scripture tells us he knows our pain and weaknesses. Jesus knows intimately how our hearts ache and how our minds are tormented. He is not a statue or mythological character who can never identify with what we have endured. We are to believe in him as God's only Son. Jesus gave his life so we could live not just on this earth but in Heaven with the Father, with him as the Son, and with the Holy Spirit. Jesus did this so we could live eternally with all our loved ones who have gone before us and have died while in a relationship with him.

On the day when Jenn got out of bed, we had our hallelujah time. We rejoiced internally and breathed externally. It was a memorable experience. It provided us with a glimmer of hope. We were able to start believing our family would make it through. The exhilaration started slowly and continued to grow each day. Martha was able to see the resurrection of her brother Lazarus, and we were able to see the resurrection, of sorts, of Jenn. But even more, we saw the resurrection of our family. On the anniversary of Miles' stillbirth, our family spent a vacation together. We laughed, cried, and sang "Happy Birthday" to Miles. We shared what this journey meant to each of us and how it changed us and altered our thought processes. Jenn and Gerald shared. Kendall and Pamela shared. Kathy and I shared. But then, of all things, Michael and Noah shared. And in their sharing, we cried, we hugged, we giggled, and then we ate cake. But above all, we began a new journey—a journey of healing. We connected once again to the goodness of God and his grace. We spoke more of the gratitude we felt than the grief we experienced and found a reason to have hope again and to live with laughter over sorrow. As King David said, "Weeping may last through the night, but joy comes in the morning" (Psalm 30:5, NLT). We aren't fully there yet, and we may never be, but for now, we are finding joy.

By saying this, my continual hope and prayer are for the families who have yet to experience this kind of recovery.

Every person having grieved for any reason needs to find hope again. They need to know it is okay to live and laugh again. They need to be able to love life and people again. Grief and sorrow can cause bitterness and loss of hope. Our family wants you to know your story doesn't have to end with the death of your loved one. Your story can find a new chapter to write as you rediscover hope in living. For us, our hope was in Christ. And maybe there was a little too much Jesus in the book for you. But we live by this foundational truth of his love for us. When we don't know what else to do, where to turn, or what is happening, we know we have Christ. When we are unsure of life's twists and turns, we know we have Jesus.

We move on in life with this knowledge base. This is how I move on. This is also my comfort—my "even now I know" mentality. I know there will be a day the vision I had of Miles will become a reality. Recognizing, responding, and living in the reality of God's love presents us with an eternal opportunity to have all this pain and sorrow wiped away. It gives us hope, knowing our suffering will last only for so long before the suffering, heartache, agony, or anger abate. Pain and loss will continue to be a part of this life; only in Christ can we find this kind of comfort from our sadness.

God loves you, he loves me, and he loves Miles. I have learned, over the years and through Miles, there is a God in Heaven. He is with us beyond time and space in our joy and pain. He is with us to heal and help. I learned this years ago, but I've had to relearn some things recently. In both cases, I have come to this conclusion: God is the same, always, in high and low situations. He is always faithful and caring. God will be there for you in your pain, just as he has been in ours. This is not my guarantee to you. It is his promise based on his word. *Even now I* know.

APPENDIX

From a Mother's Heart

As alluded to earlier, our daughter Jenn is a news anchor in Columbus, Ohio. When she was pregnant with both Noah and Harper, it was newsworthy because she was on-air, and viewers were able to see her progression during the pregnancy. They were also able to enjoy the celebration of life and birth with her as well. She would give regular updates during her maternity on social media, and her colleagues would update viewers on-air during their newscasts. The same held true when she became pregnant with Miles. However, there was no celebration of birth, only the admission of her loss. Following are her exact words both during the challenging year of 2021 and the subsequent year of his birthday and anniversary of 2022.

IN HER OWN WORDS (Written October 13, 2021)

I wish this could be a happy post . . . about the joy and excitement surrounding the birth of our son. But it's not.

On Sunday, October 10, my husband and I were told, at thirty-three weeks of pregnancy, that our son fell asleep in my womb and would not wake up. His heart stopped beating, and his soul took the journey to Heaven. Then, at 2:00 a.m., Monday, October 11, he was delivered via C-section.

Miles Owen. Three pounds, nine ounces, seventeen inches long. And he was absolutely beautiful. All of his tiny features were so perfect. But there was no breath in his lungs and no rhythm in his heart.

Shortly after his quiet birth, I was told that the placenta was attached to my uterus. And in order to save *my* life, I had to undergo a total hysterectomy. My husband and I had to come to grips with the fact that growing our family in the future, at least biologically, would no longer be an option for us . . . at just thirty-two years old.

The physical, mental, and emotional pain has been overwhelming. We don't know why this happened. There were no indications that anything was wrong. But as my husband told me, for some reason, this is part of our journey. God called our son to a much higher purpose. I may not truly understand it on this side of Heaven, but I've already witnessed the profound impact he's made on the lives of people around him.

Miles means soldier, and it's comforting to know that we have a warrior on our side in Heaven, fighting for us, protecting us, and guiding us forward.

As hard as this is, our spirits are at peace. We're grounded in our faith. And we know that this isn't forever; it's just for now. But someday, it *will* be forever when we're one big happy family once again, for all eternity.

We love our sweet baby boy—our son, brother, grandson, nephew, and cousin. He will always be a part of everything we do. We will continually honor his life. If Miles taught us anything, it's loving each other as hard as we can for as long as we can.

I know this is going to be a lifelong process. The pain will never truly go away. We will always miss him. But I know, little by little, each and every day, our little soldier will give us the strength to keep marching forward until we meet once again.

I'm going to take some time away from work, social media, and obligations to be with my family and to try to heal. Please keep us in your prayers as we navigate this. And please, *please,* honor our sweet boy by loving *your* loved ones as hard as you can for as long as you can.

November 23, 2021

Today is a tough day. Today, November 23, is the day we had been looking forward to. It was Miles Owen's due date. Instead, he was born silently on October 11. The last several weeks have been a rollercoaster. Some days I'm filled with hope, looking forward to seeing him full of life in Heaven . . . I'm able to find joy in ordinary moments. On other days, like today, it's tough to get out of bed and imagine moving forward in this life without him here. Because of my faith, I know the truth . . . but even Jesus wept over the death of his friend. And if Jesus cried, I think it's acceptable for me, too. There are some days when it just hurts. My heart physically hurts . . . but I keep it to myself and manage to put a smile on my face. Those days are the hardest. When the world around me moves on as normal, all I want to do is scream. When people want to share their pain or problems with me, all I can think is, *Are you kidding me? Do you know what I'm feeling every second of every day?* Instead, I just keep smiling. I know I can't quit. I have to keep going for *all* of my kids. This is going to be a lifelong journey. I know God is faithful and will continue to be through it all. That doesn't mean the sadness or grief just disappears. But it gives me another reason to keep moving forward. To keep loving my family as hard as I can while I have them. And to do everything I can to see my sweet boy again.

December 24, 2021

It's been a tough week, with lots of mixed emotions. Christmas is my favorite time of the year, but there have been several days when I haven't felt so jolly. I'm so looking forward to Noah and Harper opening their gifts and seeing the joy on their faces when they see that Santa brought what they asked for. I'm looking forward to the time spent with my family. But I so badly wish Miles could be here . . . I thought he *would* be here. And sometimes, those thoughts fill me with overwhelming sadness and pain.

But I know he wouldn't want me to dwell on what could have been, but instead, to stay in the present. So, I'm trying to take it moment by moment, minute by minute, recognizing the happy times when they come. I know he'll be with us on Christmas . . . not in the way I expected, but he'll be here. He'll see how crazy his brother, sister, and cousin are, and I'm sure he'll laugh along with us 🖤

So, here's to all of you who are struggling a little this Christmas season. It may not be the most wonderful time of the year for you. Just remember to take it moment by moment, minute by minute, and recognize and dwell in the happy moments when they come ♠💜🤍🖤

October 1, 2022

October is Pregnancy and Infant Loss Awareness Month. Unfortunately, not many people are aware of that unless they've been directly affected.

It's fitting, too, because October happens to be the month we lost our baby boy, Miles Owen, at thirty-three weeks. The first anniversary of his death is coming up. The last year has been really hard, but the last few weeks have been especially emotional for me. Knowing that date is approaching, I remember so vividly every detail of that day when the doctor told me Miles' heart wasn't beating. I can't even lie in bed at night without seeing and hearing it all over again. Then yesterday, this post popped up on my Facebook memories. It was like all the oxygen was sucked out of the room.

Life hasn't been the same since October 11, 2021. There have been good moments, great and joyful moments, of course, but that day changed me. I don't know if people really know just how much it did. I've become really good at suppressing and smiling in public spaces, at work, and at events, but there's so much more happening under the surface. Miles took a piece of my heart with him. I know I'll be with him again someday, but that doesn't make it all better. I miss my baby and everything he could have been.

So, do me a favor. If you take nothing else from this, please stop and consider the fact that someone you know could be carrying a bigger burden than you know or realize. Be sensitive in your words and compassionate in your actions. And when you tuck yourself in for the night, say a prayer, think a kind thought, and send lots of love to grieving and heartbroken mamas (and dads) of forever babies all over the world. 🤍

#infantloss #infantlossawareness #MilesOwen #stillbirth #stillbornstillloved

October 11, 2022

I'm usually much better at expressing my feelings in a post like this. But today is different. I've tried about ten times to say the perfect thing about my baby boy, about losing him suddenly and unexpectedly, about trying to manage the pain, grief, and depression in the 365 days since. But I don't know what to say or how to say it. One year later, I miss my boy more than ever. It still hurts. I'm still confused. I tell him, "Mommy's sorry," and "We'll be together soon." I still cry over an unplanned but life-saving hysterectomy, as crazy as that feels to say and remind myself that there's a reason for that horrible day a year ago, that there's a greater purpose. I don't know what that is yet, but I have to believe there is.

I'm grateful to everyone who's thought of my family and prayed for us over the last year. And for those of you who have shared your stillbirth stories with me. I wish we never had to live with this pain. The only thing that gives me peace is knowing that it's temporary.

My family has been my rock since Miles Owen made his journey to Heaven. I'm spending the week away with them, enjoying our time with each other in love and support, honoring and remembering our sweet boy. I know he was smiling down at us today. He has a way of letting me know that he's with us. And when I feel I'm at my weakest, he reminds me that he's there . . . that my grief is only temporary. That doesn't make it hurt any less, but it does help me to keep moving forward. Until we meet again, baby boy, I'll never not think of you. I'll say your name every day. I love you. 🤍

Miles' Mission

I have heard it said that from our pain comes purpose. In losing Miles and in the subsequent months of learning how to breathe again, we, our entire family, wanted to honor him in some way. The desire to honor him then resulted in the formation of Miles' Mission.

Through collaboration with Hands of Faith Church, Miles' Mission has at its core the belief in faith and family. Faith is an integral part of our entire family. Part of the purpose of Miles' Mission is to introduce our belief in Christ to any who will hear. We also believe strongly in the family structure and desire to help others to find the same support system that exists in all our homes as well.

The loss of stillborn children affects more than twenty-six thousand families annually in the United States and over 2.6 million worldwide. It is quickly becoming a topic of discussion for politicians at the national, state, and local levels. It is also gaining traction in the health industry through hospitals recognizing the many patients they are attending to, and it is being recognized by mental health agencies to treat such issues as depression, PTSD, and post-partum struggles. These situations continue to escalate in women, men, and extended family members who have been heartbroken after experiencing such a loss.

With the experiences and renewal of hope as part of our family's healing, we desire to be a voice for those families and babies to further the cause of having better medical benefits, more access to mental health assistance, and reminding faith-based organizations, including churches, of our mission to bring spiritual healing to all.

It is our hope Miles' Mission will operate as an organization assisting businesses, mental health and physical health agencies, and faith-based entities in collaborating and working towards bettering our communities. We strive to do our best in connecting these organizations to help in the wellness (mental health), wholeness (social awareness), and oneness (spiritual well-being) of individuals in need. This is for both public and private agencies and corporations.

For more information on Miles' Mission, please visit our website at MilesMission.com.

Notes

Cambridge Dictionary. s.v. "guilt." Accessed April 20, 2023. https://dictionary.cambridge.org/dictionary/english/guilt.

Cambridge Dictionary. s.v., "profound." Accessed April 20, 2023. https://dictionary.cambridge.org/dictionary/english/profound.

Acknowledgments

Without hesitation, when it comes to acknowledging anyone, first and foremost on my list of earthly people is my wife, Kathy. The most amazing woman, friend, mother, grandmother, and person I have ever known. Her inspiration, encouragement, and unconditional love have meant more to me than the air I breathe. Your prayers, wisdom, and grace are a testament to God's Spirit in and on you, as you have been the strength of our family for all these years.

To my girls, Pamela and Jennifer, outside of your mom, I am both honored and humbled to be your daddy. You made me proud the moment I first held you in the maternity room, and you have made me proud every day since. You are both as amazing as your mom and an inspiration to so many. Your strength, courage, spirit, and intellect are only outshined by how beautiful you both are inside and out. You are both incredible warriors for God's kingdom.

To my sons-in-law, Kendall and Gerald, who have been wonderful support systems to my girls. Thank you for allowing them to stay connected to their family and for always being there in whatever adventures they dragged you to. Also, thank you for being wonderful dads to our grandbabies. Watching you both grow and mature has been a privilege, and I am proud to be in your lives. To our church family, thank you for your support, patience, prayers, and encouragement. You are the most wonderful people whom we consider family. Kathy and I are honored beyond measure to pastor such outstanding people who have made a profound impact on the Kingdom of God. A special thank you to those women who politely and lovingly shared their stories of sorrow, brokenness, and grief. You are as much a part of this as anything.

To my mentors, both past and present, my father-in-law and mother-in-law, Cecil 'Dean' (deceased), and Yvonne Tabler, you were my first pastor and the inspiration for me to further my education, thank you. To Dr. Jerry Fryar, Dr. Sam Huddleston, Pastor Lois Hoshor, Mel Kurtz, and Pastor Steve Harrop, your lives, your input, and your instruction have been invaluable in my development, and I truly appreciate each of you and the gifts you bring to my life and the kingdom. And not last because of importance, but last because of the foundation of all that I am and for everything that has transpired, I thank the Lord God Almighty for this life you have called me to. Even in the greatest of pain, you have been my God, and in the greatest of joy, I have seen life anew. Thank you for your words within these pages, and thank you for the love of your Son, my Lord and Savior, Jesus Christ.

About the Author

Dr. Michael Bullock is the senior pastor of Hands of Faith Church in Zanesville, Ohio, a ministry he and his wife Kathy established. Along with his family, he recently founded Miles' Mission: a ministry that strives to connect organizations, government agencies, and the faith-based community to assist in the development of the mental, physical, and spiritual health of all individuals in need.

He is a native of Columbus, Ohio, and holds a bachelor of science in Business Management from Franklin

University, an ABS certification in Biblical Studies, and a master of ministry degree from Moody Bible Institute in Chicago. Later on, he earned a doctor of ministry from Regent University in Chesapeake, Virginia.

Having received his call to ministry in 1983, he was ordained in 1989 under the Reverend Cecil E. Tabler. During his career, he has served as a youth director, assistant pastor, and founding pastor of Hands of Faith Church. The church has seen consistent and stable growth over the years and impacted the Southeastern and Central Ohio regions.

Dr. Bullock works tirelessly for his community, serving as a board member for Muskingum County Adult and Child Protective Services, the Salvation Army, Fellowship of Christians Athletes, City of Zanesville Historical Zoning Board, Trulight Ministries, Genesis Healthcare Advisory Board, and the Governor's Evangelical Advisory Council.

For twenty-two years, he was a head varsity coach at three high schools, coaching boys and girls in basketball, track and field, and cross country, and girls' tennis. He was awarded Coach of the Year honors eight times and received several league commendations, in addition to participating in state championship teams and coaching All Ohio athletes and others who continued their athletic careers in college.

Dr. Bullock has spoken at seminars and conferences and hosted various radio and television programs, and his articles have appeared in local and national publications. He has traveled throughout the United States, Africa, and Haiti to share the gospel of Jesus Christ.

He married his beloved Kathy in 1983 and shares with her the joy of having two daughters, Pamela (Kendall) Stevens and Jennifer (Gerald) Moore, and six grandchildren, Ka'Niyah, Michael, and Jakobi Stevens; and Noah, Harper, and Miles (deceased) Moore.

About Miles' Mission

Vision Statement

Our vision is to impact lives through a collaborative effort between faith-based and community organizations.

It is our hope Miles' Mission will operate as an organization that assists businesses, mental health and physical health agencies, and faith-based entities to collaborate and work towards bettering our communities. We strive to do our best to connect these organizations together to help in the wellness (mental health), wholeness (social awareness), and oneness (spiritual well-being) of individuals in need. This is for both public and private agencies and corporations.

Mission Statement

Our mission is to provide hope for those hurting, to help those grieving, and to present future opportunities to area youth.

Miles' Mission desires to help individuals who are hurting due to loneliness, depression, anxiety, and struggles with life issues.

Furthermore, our mission to reach those grieving will be primarily for women or families of stillborn children. We know many wonderful organizations and agencies exist to provide counseling for other areas of grief, but there are too few organizations that deal with stillbirth loss. We hope to bring the grief-stricken together with organizations that have developed counseling curricula to aid in the mental health of the bereaved.

We also want to be a conduit for aiding our area's young people in finding a purpose for their future through career opportunities, whether in a four-year institution or the trade industry and to collaborate with agencies in mentorship programs to aid in developing relationships with our youth as well. We do this for all the stillborn babies whose futures have been cut short.

MICHAEL WANTS TO CONNECT WITH YOU

Follow him on your favorite social media platforms.

Miles' Mission
for those who grieve

HOPE FOR THE HURTING
HELP FOR THE GRIEVING
A FUTURE FOR THE YOUNG

milesmission.com

THIS BOOK IS PROTECTED INTELLECTUAL PROPERTY

The author of this book values Intellectual Property. The book you just read is protected by Easy IP™, a proprietary process, which integrates blockchain technology giving Intellectual Property "Global Protection." By creating a "Time-Stamped" smart contract that can never be tampered with or changed, we establish "First Use" that tracks back to the author.

Easy IP™ functions much like a Pre-Patent™ since it provides an immutable "First Use" of the Intellectual Property. This is achieved through our proprietary process of leveraging blockchain technology and smart contracts. As a result, proving "First Use" is simple through a global and verifiable smart contract. By protecting intellectual property with blockchain technology and smart contracts, we establish a "First to File" event.

Powered By Easy IP™

LEARN MORE AT EASYIP.TODAY